# THE BACK HOME SERIES

Series Titles

**Matrix**

Live at Lawrence Chapel | Appleton, WI – March 10, 1979

# From the Heart

## THE STORY OF MATRIX

## JOHN HARMON

CORNERSTONE PRESS
UNIVERSITY OF WISCONSIN-STEVENS POINT

Cornerstone Press, Stevens Point, Wisconsin 54481
Copyright © 2023 John Harmon
www.uwsp.edu/cornerstone

Printed in the United States of America by
Point Print and Design Studio, Stevens Point, Wisconsin

Library of Congress Control Number: 2023944672
ISBN: 978-1-960329-14-1

Cover Photo: Matrix in Salt Lake City, ca. 1977

This is a work of nonfiction. All of the events in this book are true to the best of the author's memory. Some names and identifying features have been changed to protect the identity of certain parties. The author in no way represents any company, corporation, or brand, mentioned herein. The views expressed in this memoir are solely those of the author.

Cornerstone Press titles are produced in courses and internships offered by the Department of English at the University of Wisconsin–Stevens Point.

DIRECTOR & PUBLISHER
Dr. Ross K. Tangedal

EXECUTIVE EDITOR
Jeff Snowbarger

EDITORIAL DIRECTOR
Brett Hill

SENIOR EDITOR
Grace Dahl

PRESS STAFF
Ellie Atkinson, Carolyn Czerwinski, Grace Dahl, Zoie Dinehart, Kirsten Faulkner, Kenzie Kierstyn, Brett Hill, Natalie Reiter, Lauren Rudesill, Catriona Scheinost, Anthony Theil

*This book is humbly dedicated to the memory of passionate jazz advocate and dear friend, Mindy Cibrario. Her gentle insistence and loving persuasion resulted in the realization of this narrative.*

*Deep thanks, Mindy.*

*With love—*
*John and Traf*

*Matrix* (Ultra Nova, 1976)

*Matrix IX* (RCA, 1976)

*Wizard* (Warner Bros., 1978)

*Tale of the Whale* (Warner Bros., 1979)

*Harvest* (Pablo Today, 1979)

*Proud Flesh* (Summit Records, 2002)

# Contents

# Foreword

John Harmon knew the musical statement he wanted to make to the world. To do this he needed opportunity; he needed determination; and he needed musicians who shared his philosophy with the expertise to execute his vision. In short, he needed a miracle!

In 1974, these elements came together and the musical experiment called Matrix found its voice. *And what a voice it was!*

Matrix spoke with a voice filled with joy, energy, and originality that captivated music lovers and critics alike. A voice like theirs had never before been heard. It was a shared philosophy expressed in notes. Their music was a true collaboration: each man committing to the adventure, each man contributing to the whole

As the music evolved, it continued to build and expand. There was no perceived destination, no assurance that it would be understood, and no guarantee that it would be appreciated. No matter. They were committed to integrity, excellence, and respect for their audience. Musically, they extended their hand, trusting the audience to reach out and grasp the beauty and honesty of their music.

It's clear that when you see these men together today, they share a bond *far stronger* than friendship: they share the same values; they share the same pride; they share a loyalty that can only be achieved through having tested themselves. Together, they shared and achieved the same vision. They *created* the legacy of Matrix: one of excellence, invention, and collaboration.

Over the years, stories of Matrix have been shared and appreciated by loyal fans. Family and friends have repeatedly urged John to share these memories in a book. He always declined. He simply wasn't ready.

But, one summer night, John and Traf, my husband, Dan, and I were sitting at a table sipping a drink and enjoying our dinner. The conversation turned to a memory of Matrix that even Traf hadn't heard. When John had finished his recollection, we were all silent for a moment. Finally, we all begged, "Please consider writing a book. The story is so unique and incredibly moving! But *you* need to tell it. It needs to be told in your own voice."

A pause…a smile. To our shock and amazement, he said, "You're right. I'll do it!" So here it is.

All it took was forty-five years, four friends gathered around a table, and four perfect gimlets!

—Mindy Cibrario
Appleton, Wisconsin

# From the Heart

## The Story of Matrix

# 1

*Elmhurst College, Illinois*
*March 18, 1973*

"And this year's winner is . . . the very fine band from Lawrence."

—Chuck Suber, publisher of *DownBeat*

Little did I know at the time, but that simple declaration planted a seed that would one day, in the not-too-distant future, bring forth a flower that would change the lives of nine very naïve, courageous, adventuresome, and truly dedicated young men.

The occasion was the final playoff for collegiate jazz bands that were competing for the right to represent the Midwest in what was called the National Collegiate Jazz Festival.

Participating bands came from Wisconsin, Minnesota, Michigan, Indiana, Illinois, and Iowa. The winner would receive an all-expense paid trip to this year's location (McCormick Place, Chicago, IL) and perform there.

Other regional winners would perform at their own appointed time slots but because the LUJE (Lawrence University Jazz Ensemble) earned the same number of points as Eau Claire, a coin toss (just like football) determined who would play first. Lawrence University won the toss and chose to perform after Eau Claire.

While everyone anxiously awaited the final decision by the judges of the playoff between Lawrence University and the University of Wisconsin–Eau Claire, Cannonball Adderley delivered an elegant treatise on the challenges and rewards of jazz excellence. This is an excerpt from his talk:

> "It is a very precious dilemma to try to figure out who is the best. Because there is no such thing as the best. Unfortunately, competition is…you know, we're not combatants in a tournament. We are musicians seeking honest professional evaluation from someone for whom we allegedly have respect."

He went on to say, "Thank God, and thank all those who have participated here for being as great as you have been and for making this experience a rewarding one."

It was later reprinted in its entirety in *DownBeat*. It was a stunning footnote to an already stunning experience for all of us! We, the Lawrence University Jazz Ensemble, had just won the damned thing! And we didn't even have a 'bass' player (Bob Hanisch played Fender Rhodes 'bass' with his left hand)!

But what we did have was one killer brass section! That's not to imply that the rest of the players weren't great, because they certainly were. I'm talking about our brass players who were a flat-out, kick-ass professional-sounding group.

As exhilarating as the afterglow of our winning performance was, something noteworthy occurred that deserves mention: the panel of judges included such luminaries as David Baker, Rufus Reid, Nathan Davis, Rich Matteson, and the aforementioned Chuck Suber. Heading this prestigious group was the great Cannonball Adderly!

So, the drive back to Appleton, Wisconsin, from Elmhurst, Illinois, with drummer Tony Wagner, was spent in euphoric, celebratory conversation that made the three-hour-plus trip seem like nothing. The only drag was that on the way back all the bars were closed due to the late hour… and in those days, we lived on beer.

No matter; what I had witnessed as their director was growth, dedication, and deep passion for making music. All of this got filed away in my subconscious and would come to the fore down the line.

The seed had been sown on that chilly March night.

# 2

After our triumph in Elmhurst, I guess I was a little disappointed that there wasn't a bit more hoopla over the accomplishment of this remarkable group and what they had done for the school's reputation.

No matter; we had much bigger fish to fry. In mid-June, school was already out and we had to get ready for the National Collegiate Jazz Festival in Chicago!

Before taking the gig as Director of Jazz Studies, I'd never stood in front of a big band…ever! And now, we were preparing to play for some of the heaviest of heavies and hundreds of knowledgeable jazz enthusiasts.

Scared the living shit out of me, to tell the truth! But I got over it thanks to the bond that had been forged between myself and members of the band. My confidence was especially buoyed by the profoundly great musicianship of these young players!

Hell, I was just another cut-above-the-average jazz pianist with one recording to my credit, albeit with the great Yusef Lateef (And, incidentally, they misspelled my name as Hormon in the liner notes!).

These gifted young people could play anything that was put in front of them! I so envied and admired that skill, since bad vision left me a poor sight reader. Between my admiration for their skills and the affection I felt for them, I got over my insecurities.

Even though school was officially out, all the members of the Lawrence University Jazz Ensemble (LUJE) were more than happy to stick around and perhaps even forego a summer job and get ready for the upcoming event in Chicago. And we got ready.

Boy, did we get ready! The intensity level of rehearsals was kicked up a notch, and the playing elevated to a new level.

When it came time for the festival, I felt pretty confident; our group rewarded my confidence with what Jimmy Lyons, host of the festival, described as 'an electrifying performance.' His enthusiasm for that memorable showing would turn out to be important down the line.

Later in the summer I moved in with the drummer of the band, Tony Wagner, a fine player and friend. I had just separated from my wife of ten years so Tony's willingness to let me share his pad was a real godsend.

Tony and I had a small group: piano, bass, drums, and guitar. Lee Kusserow played bass, and the guitar chair was held down by an amazing guitarist, one Dave Sullivan! My oh my, this dude could lay it down!

It was a pretty fun group. We were fortunate to have a regular weekly gig in downtown Appleton at a place called J.W. Puddy. So, on nights we weren't playing, Puddy's became our hang.

Hanging out at Puddy's I got to meet one of Tony's friends: Mark Stenz, a chubby little guy with a lot of smarts and what appeared to be a love of jazz. We quickly became friends and did a lot of "Puddy hang time." He was a divorcee with a young daughter, Karianne.

I suppose my shaky marriage fed into some of the camaraderie we shared through our failed marriages. He was funny as hell and fun to be around.

One of the young owners, Tom Andrew, liked the band, and, as summer unfolded, we became good friends. I'll always be grateful for his support and friendship. Anyway, it was probably late July and I was at Puddy's with Tony and Mark.

I'd been extolling the brilliance of our college brass section and bemoaning the fact that it would all disappear once school was over and it hit me like a bolt of lightning!

Suddenly, I just blurted: "It doesn't have to be over! I'm gonna form an experimental group, write a bunch of new shit and tour and record! And it's gonna be called…Matrix! And I'm gonna use the core of these guys in the LUJE!"

I'm sure there was a lot of 'beer talk' there, but I was dead serious! My enthusiasm rubbed off on my friends so, though I don't remember, I'm pretty sure there were more beers ordered!

What I *do* recall though was a lot of clinking of glasses toasting the concept of Matrix! *Phew!* I can still feel that excitement! Matrix! Yeah!

# 3

The next day Tony was quick to remind me of my 'declaration' from the night before and essentially admonish me should I show any hint of cold feet. I reassured him that I was committed to the idea. Actually, I was serious to the point of obsession!

My original vision was for a fourteen piece 'little' big band. But Tony, ever financially pragmatic, opted for a seven-piece group. Because of purely musical preferences (orchestration-wise) I held my ground.

Eventually, after considering the booking headache for such a large number, we settled on nine players which also took into account the guys from the LUJE who we wanted to recruit.

We quickly went to work filling in the names. "Okay. We gotta have Fred!" (Sturm), bass trombone and phenomenal composer/arranger. First pick!

Mike Hale (Tex) was a must because of his Maynard-like range and jazz chops! Lead trumpet for sure!

Next, Jeff Pietrangelo (Chimp), virtuosic trumpet technique, great improviser, range enough to spell Tex from time to time, lovable personality, overall brilliant musician! A must.

Next, Larry Darling (Zap) trumpet! The most versatile, natural player I'd ever met: great intuitive improviser, wonderful lead singer-type voice, synthesizer wizard, sensitive section player, and a bit of a perfectionist with great relative pitch! Gotta have him!

Kurt Dietrich, aka Dietch (pronounced "Deetch")– beautiful trombone sound, lyrical soloist, dry sense of humor, wonderfully organized, disciplined, a perfect match to blend with Fred.

Obviously, Tony would take care of the drums and I would be keyboard/composer. What about bass? As stated earlier, we didn't have a bass player in LUJE so it would be a critical hole to fill as far as this dream band.

As it turns out, Tony knew a bass player in a fairly well-known local rock band called Taylor. His name was Randal Fird. Not only was he a solid bass player; he was also a fine singer. So, Tony approached Randal and he agreed to give it a go.

We now had eight players. My composer/arranger brain was crying for a versatile reed player who could double on flute, alto and tenor saxes. That problem would be faced later.

No students were around in July because it was summer vacation. School wouldn't be in session for another month or so, but I was pretty hot to get going and anxious to at least contact the guys we had decided on.

Both Fred and Dietch, having graduated, were going on to their respective graduate programs. Fred was enrolled in the North Texas State jazz program and would be starting in the fall. He would eventually audition for, and get accepted as, a member of the famed One O'Clock Band.

Dietch was accepted into the graduate program at Northwestern University and would take up residence in Chicago with some pals from Lawrence. For the moment their invitations could wait. But I was able to contact those still at Lawrence (Tex, Chimp, Zap) and all three enthusiastically jumped at the idea.

The thought of doing forward-looking, challenging new music with close friends was a no-brainer! The enthusiasm of everyone added a new dimension of excitement! Man! This thing was actually happening! I was beside myself and couldn't wait for classes to begin!

Eventually Fred and Dietch also happily said "Yes," so we were pretty close to the full roster by the end of the first term.

# 4

"*Matrix*: A mold in which a thing is cast or developed; an environment or substance in which a thing is developed…" …this, according to the *Oxford English Dictionary*. Not a bad definition to accommodate the goals of my original idea, I'd say.

In Latin, 'matrix' also means 'mother.' 'Nuff said.

It was during the waning weeks of summer that my new friend, Mark Stenz, (mentioned earlier) got as excited about the project as the players. He was a very street-wise guy and, at the time, seemed the perfect fit as someone to manage the group. Plus, Tony and I got along with him really well. As I said, funny, quirky sense of humor, savvy in the ways of the world.

Little did we know of the sort of blurred lines between the fundamental difference between right and wrong, something we would find out later. His nickname was 'Turd.' Where that came from, I couldn't tell you, but that was it.

When school reconvened in September, those whom we had contacted were gifted ID bracelets with Matrix proudly engraved on them. It almost had the feeling of a secret club at first but soon, everyone around knew of our plans.

In the meantime, as school progressed, the missing reed player emerged in the person of Michael Bard, a hot-shot graduate of Evanston Township High School. His band director was Don Owens, a fairly well-known jazz educator.

I know that Michael spoke very highly of him. I believe Owens's jazz program was one of the better ones in the Midwest. He would later head up the graduate jazz program at Northwestern University.

Michael had a very good sense of jazz style and was versatile: flute, soprano, alto, and tenor saxes; he was also an excellent sight reader, and very confident with a leader mentality. At times, to be honest, he seemed a bit too sure of himself. But he was 'all in' when we approached him. So that filled out the instrumental roster needs.

And, to the disbelief of some observers, *no guitar!* "This is not going to be a flippin' rock band!" was my response to any nay-sayers. We had much bigger musical fish to fry.

# 5

The school year progressed more quickly than I realized, mainly due to my very demanding schedule as Director of Jazz Studies. And of course, there were the activities of preparation for Matrix. I had, by the beginning of the school year, already decided on not returning to Lawrence in the fall of '74. No chance.

For whatever the future held, Matrix was my ultimate motivation, my *raison d'etre!* I would often lay awake half the night planning, dreaming, totally consumed with the idea of Matrix!

But naturally, in the harsh light of day, there was much, much to do! The idea of sustaining nine people presented some sobering realities to tackle. It became obvious that to survive we needed a cover book (current pop songs).

My musical experience was pretty narrow; as a jazz performer and classical composer, I was a post be-bop piano player with a master's degree in Composition. Hmm... my knowledge of the pop arena was limited at best.

Guess what? I had eight other guys who knew all this! They were brought up on it! So the plan turned into assignments for all of them to transcribe the latest reasonable pop rock that would be fun to put our spin on. With a couple of dozen or so horn band charts of pop stuff, we'd be ready to earn enough bread to survive.

What an education for me: Captain & Tennille, Tower of Power, The Beatles, Marvin Gaye, Elton John, Led Zeppelin. Whew! Two of the more important groups we 'covered' were Blood, Sweat and Tears, and Chicago! Both of these groups had some jazz leanings and I actually knew of them! They both had huge hits like "Spinning Wheel" and "Does Anybody Really Know What Time It Is?"

At one point there was an unforgettable one-time-only vocal rendering of Chimp singing "Color My World." You can guess why it was a one-time-only performance…I'm sorry there's no recording of it because if one ever needed a laugh, that would certainly do the trick!

I wrote a few arrangements of tunes that leaned more toward jazz, but my primary job was to start the real book: the stuff we all hungered to sink our collective teeth into! It was one hell of a learning experience for me, their so-called director. I was around thirty-eight at the time and these guys were all in their early twenties.

As I tried to get the hang of some of this 'repertoire,' it was a classic case of the *bleeping* tail wagging the dog! As it turned out, they were pretty tolerant of my lack of experience in the pop arena. Frankly, it was quite an education for the old fart!

Actually, at the time, I was leading a trio, The John Harmon Trio, with bassist, Lee Kusserow, and drummer/singer Dan Peterson. Dan's repertoire included some of the pop hits of the day. I just simply didn't know a lot of the current music of the groups our Matrix guys favored to include.

Truthfully, I preferred more sophisticated music genres: bop, classical, etc. but I was certainly in favor of including all the styles that would help keep us afloat until we could declare our "independence."

By this time, as graduation neared, pretty much everyone knew of the musical entity, Matrix. It was either Phi Mu Alpha Sinfonia or some other student activity group that sponsored an actual date for Matrix to perform.

But here's the ironic kicker: the site of the gig was to be the Lawrence Memorial Union.

\* \* \* \* \*

*Guess what? This is actual fact: almost twenty years earlier, in May of 1955, the very first jazz concert on the Lawrence campus was held at Lawrence Memorial Union.*

*It was headed up by Lawrence undergraduate…you guessed it, "Yours Truly"!! The group included a trumpet player named Jerry Dunn, with bassist Jerry Rusch, and a drummer, whose name, I believe, was Jack Kortie.*

*In the fifties, jazz was not considered acceptable music by the conservatory. I personally had to jump through a bunch of flaming hoops to schedule a space for the event, but I finally got clearance.*

\* \* \* \* \*

But here we are, in 1974, nearly twenty years later, about to launch the musical ship, Matrix! and…in the very same venue as my first naive attempt to present jazz in concert.

Enough to raise some goosebumps, don't you think?

# 6

You know how it is as a kid in anticipation of Christmas? The hopes, laughter, doubts (was I a good boy?) and absolute, unbridled excitement! And then the moment finally arrived:

"Tonight. On behalf of the Lawrence Memorial Union, Phi Mu Alpha Sinfonia is proud to present, for their very first performance, home grown right on this campus; put your hands together for the exciting new band, Matrix!!"

Oh my god! It was an unbelievable rush to hear that intro after months of anticipation! Before the raucous applause had died down, we launched into Tower of Power's iconic hit, "What Is Hip!" It was probably the perfect cover to initiate our maiden voyage. First tune, first gig! I shall never forget the high that this momentous occasion prompted. It was actually happening!

And to add to the inner excitement, the crowd went wonderfully crazy, especially the women students, when Zap or Randal sang; both guys were "hotties" in the eyes of the fairer sex! It was one hell of a night! I, as a jazz pianist, had never received this kind of response. Of course, with students in the group not yet graduated, all their pals were giving them enthusiastic support beyond the norm. No matter. The thrill was memorable.

The only drag for me was the stack of charts I had to struggle through. Reading music was never my long suit. As a jazz guy, my repertoire was all in my head, memorized. So, this was a totally new world I was entering and actually, despite my deficiencies, that aspect was exciting, too! The old-dog-new-tricks cliché be damned!

All in all, our first gig was an unqualified success, and we were all pretty pleased. Hell, we were ecstatic! Who am I kidding?

# 7

Our next gig was the following night, June 1, 1974, at our favorite hangout, J.W. Puddy. School was still in session and I still had the usual last-term mop up: grading papers, exams, etc. but my tenure as Director of Jazz Studies was nearly over; my marriage pretty much over as well. What the hell did I have to be concerned with other than this dream band? 'All in' is the term that applied to my life at this point.

I fully embraced the idea of a creative life with nothing close to an understanding of the challenges that perhaps lay ahead. No matter. The idyllic dream was happening and that's all I saw or cared about.

Still pretty sky-high from the triumph of our first performance, the Puddy gig should be a positive slam dunk. And it was!

Somehow, we crammed all of us (and gear) into an inadequate space. There was no stage. The bar was kind of long, and the band was jammed against the back wall as they played. Plus, there was a pillar they had to work around!

No matter, we were working! And in very comfortable, (except for cramped quarters) supportive surroundings. The place was totally packed with well-wishers, fans, curiosity seekers. The word was on the street and people wanted to check us out. "Who are these guys?" "What are they all about?" Even though we were doing covers, our instrumentation and, of course, our arrangements set us apart from the usual guitar-based regional groups.

Furthermore…and this was the big one…a serious commitment to improvisation with a strong jazz influence. As one keyboard player from a local cover band said, "You guys are breaking all the rules!" And of course, included in our performance was the truly fine musicianship in the rendering of what amounted to 'pop' standards; we created unique arrangements with unusual instrumentation.

I mean, come on; three trumpets, two bones, one reed, and three rhythm. And no guitar. Pretty outrageous in the pop-rock arena!!

In the meantime, Turd was doing his thing and managed to secure a three-week stint at the Embassy Suites Motor Lodge on the west side of Appleton. Right in our backyard, for heaven's sake! This wasn't a Phi Mu gift, or Puddy's, but an actual professional gig! A house gig for three weeks! Is this cool, or what!?!

The bread (money) wasn't great, but enough to get along on, plus a chance to play every night and get acclimated to real steady work. But most importantly, it was my chance to start the real book of music; the book to define my vision; the ultimate musical direction that would define who we would become.

During the day the bandstand at the Embassy was available to us. With that in mind one afternoon I went out to the site and fired up my Fender Rhodes keyboard. Maybe an hour or so later I had come up with my first real entry into 'the book.' It was titled "Balthazar," inspired by the second book in Lawrence Durrell's The Alexandria Quartet.

What makes this significant is not just that this was my first original for the band, but the idea that "Balthazar" was an attempt at program-matic music: music that paints a picture, tells a story, or creates a specific mood for the potential listener.

Programmatic pieces of the late nineteenth century told stories in music. And those stories were printed in the programs (hence the term programmatic) to help the listener understand the composer's intent. This would become our signature in the future. It would also set us apart from the norm in the country's musical landscape.

Stay tuned . . . Remember, this was the seventies, man! Summer of 1974 to be exact.

As jazz people we witnessed, with no small measure of disdain, the emergence of the new dance craze called Disco by the pop music pundits. Talk about formulaic mediocrity! Every tune at metronome marking quarter note = 120.

By contrast, at the same time, Miles Davis, a superhero to any jazz enthusiast, was into his flamboyant costumes and hip-hop. Ah, the seventies . . .

# 8

The gig at the Embassy went pretty well if memory serves me. Of course, we were playing pop covers geared to dancing, and I guess we were satisfying the club's needs in that department. Truthfully, it was kind of fun seeing us go over well even though deep down I was itching to get after it in a more musically satisfying way.

But what the hell, we were playing, having fun with each other, and actually making a little bread. Things could be better, but certainly things could be worse. So we just enjoyed the ride for what turned out to be several months.

After the Embassy, Turd got us a week-long gig at a rock joint named The Horny Bull in Mankato, Minnesota. Our first road trip! (chuckle)

As the name of the club might suggest, this place catered to the young set; what we were doing seemed to be appropriate for the room. And, like kids out of school (which I guess we were!) we partied pretty heartily. Nothing outrageous, mind you, but plenty of fun! The whole experience was new, even exciting…so let 'er rip!

One thing I do remember about the Horny Bull gig was that my sister, who lived in the Twin Cities, came one evening. Early in the first set, before the dance stuff began, we played "Balthazar." I'm not sure it was the 'premiere,' but I know my sister Anne loved it! She even confessed to tearing up after hearing it.

However, it never would have gone over during our 'regular' routine! Guaranteed!

We went back to the Fox Valley after the Horny Bull and returned to The Second Sun in Oshkosh, another college town; actually my place of birth. Musically more of the same. Rock/pop but with a big fat brass sound that people seemed to like.

Next, we did four weeks in Racine, Wisconsin at a place called the Sir Thomas Lounge. With all this time in one place it afforded me and Fred (Sturm) the opportunity to peck away at the 'good stuff.' Plus, we could try a piece out during the day without 'offending' the evening's dance-happy customers.

Following the gig in Racine, we returned to Appleton for another stint at our home course, J.W. Puddy. This was in our wheelhouse and definitely not a dance gig; it was filled with a bunch of supportive friends. But most importantly, it was a place to try out our new, meaningful stuff. Oh yeah! After that brief respite, it was back for another week at The Second Sun for more of the, let's say, less-than-meaningful stuff. But we were working.

As to the pop stuff, there were several contributors to our 'shit book', namely Zap, Tex, Michael, me, and especially Fred Sturm. The arrangements had to be adapted for six horns, while maintaining the recognizable 'hit recording' for our dance fans. But the creativity of our arrangers kept creeping into our tunes so, little by little, we were finding 'our sound.'

The exceptional skill and musical vision of Fred's thinking gave us some very 'un-pop,' sophisticated sounds. For example, he did a Beatles medley that was both clever and musically satisfying for us as players. And, as long as it was tagged 'Beatles,' we got away with it. Hell, it was so hip, I'd be happy and proud to do it today were we still performing.

Meanwhile, Turd was doing his job and scored a week-long, cool gig for us (the first of several) at a ski resort way up in the Upper Peninsula in Marquette, Michigan.

This turned out to be quite a significant booking for us as we won over the hearts of some very cool, serious jazz music lovers, as well as some fine musicians who lived up there. Perhaps, even more importantly, we forged some lifelong friendships that still mean a great deal to us today.

One couple in particular, Bob and Shirley Moore, were especially hospitable, frequently inviting the whole group for wonderful, memorable dinners. They are two of the coolest people I'm still blessed to call my friends! Bob, a former Air Force pilot in WWII, was a fine jazz trumpet player; he absolutely loved our brass section.

So, actually at the ski resort, Cliff's Ridge, we enjoyed the nightly presence of a music-loving crowd. We were able to keep growing our 'good book' and actually playing some of it without endangering the gig. Frankly, they loved us.

After our Marquette success we did a couple of school concerts, most notably a return to Lawrence University, but this time in their main performance site known as the Chapel! Things were definitely looking up.

Expanding our original book, playing some good venues, making some bread; we were feeling pretty damned good about ourselves.

# 9

I seem to remember getting a call from either a former student or someone from Appleton; it might have been a friend of one of the guys, but the main thing was that it was an invitation to play at the Institute of Technology on November 9, 1974, in Rochester, New York! Alright! New York? Bring it on!

It was a serious road trip, the money was good, and we had our book of good stuff well prepared…The excitement to showcase our new material to a truly 'virgin' audience was palpable! This is what we were working for after all. We were well-rehearsed and brimming with confidence. Let's do this thing!

After the long trek to Rochester, the moment actually arrived for our performance. We were scheduled to open for a local trio. Cool. Here we are, a nine-piece, highly charged power group opening for a trio; probably keyboard, bass and drums. After the usual sound check we were ready to go. The venue was fairly well-filled, adding to our anticipation. So, wham! Off we go!

Our set went pretty well I thought, though the response wasn't quite as enthusiastic as I had hoped. What the hell? We played well enough. Maybe the crowd wasn't quite ready for what we were offering. So, let's hear this local trio. The name of the group was Petrus featuring Phil Markowitz (keyboard), Gordon Johnson (electric bass), and a drummer whose name I don't recall.

Did I mention this was in Rochester, New York? Did I further mention Rochester—home of the Eastman School of Music? Home of some of the finest young players in the country? Uh, no. I didn't.

By the time Phil Markowitz (keyboard extraordinaire!) and his trio, which included Gordon Johnson (bass virtuoso), were doing their sound check, the place was packed!

And listening to Phil do a few licks for the sound man, the guys and I were kind of in shock! Phil had a couple of synthesizers and created some exciting new colors I'd never heard! Plus, he displayed some amazing chops (technique)! And then they got after it!

They were unbelievable, with wonderfully contemporary, original pieces that left me totally dazzled on one hand…and deflated on the other. These guys were cutting-edge fantastic (Phil and his side men went on to very fine professional careers after Eastman)! Talk about your humble pie! We packed up our gear in shocked silence after the gig, pretty much with our collective tail between our legs.

Learning from one's setbacks is what builds character I'm told. My concern was that we didn't go into the tank from our first real taste of adversity. Fusion, the mixing of acoustic and electric instruments (including synthesizer), was the new concept/style on the musical scene. Petrus gave us a level to aspire to.

So now what? We got our asses handed to us; a true gut-check moment. How do we respond? I can tell you that on that long trip back I did some hard thinking about our future. I'm sure I wasn't alone in trying to deal with a real body-blow to our collective psyche. Yes, we got our asses kicked, but by god, we weren't ready to quit!

My biggest concern was to convince everyone that we could learn from this. Perhaps things had gone too smoothly in the beginning. It was probably a much-needed dose of reality. I guess the future would tell what we were, indeed, made of.

Time did its healing thing, but soul searching went a lot further for me. Damn it all! We were going to do some ass-kicking of our own and we'd figure it out, and then... go do it!

# 10

Back in Wisconsin we had a series of 'home games' with the usual enthusiastic responses; but they kind of became the traditional 'water off the duck's back' as far as our getting cocky over such enthusiastic feedback. I can't speak for Fred, but inside I was churning: we needed better, more challenging music!

Deep down I still felt we were going to find that special niche I had dreamt of! I'm guessing Fred sensed something similar as both of us were coming up with new stuff for the 'real book.' But that takes time! So we kept doing the 'shit' gigs to provide the obvious financial needs.

We had a kind of laughable setback right before Christmas. Turd scored a really nice-paying gig for two weeks in East Lansing at a club called Dooley's near the Michigan State campus. By then we had kind of snuck a few 'real tunes' into our performances but, of course, we still had a crock of the usual cover stuff. Whatever the case, after one set, the manager of the club flatly stated to Turd, "This ain't boogie!"

You got it: we were fired after one night.

Other than the financial setback, I don't recall a whole lot of remorse in the band. It certainly seemed demeaning to have this unbelievably talented group of people have to 'dumb down' to the pop level mentality in order to stay afloat. Oh well; life in the cultural kindergarten.

The next couple of months provided some return engagements, a couple schools, and a couple dates at a place called Teddy's in Milwaukee. Teddy's was the place to break into the Milwaukee scene, so we were told. What a joke! After our performance some big booker dude asked me to join their table.

Meanwhile, the rest of the band awaited the result of this summit. The guy was so patronizing that I got thoroughly pissed as he told me we were too big, too sophisticated and, I think, too loud! Total unmitigated B.S.!

Outside, I'm sure I didn't set a good example to the group as I threw my coat onto the pavement and relayed my total exasperation from the encounter. I was so upset because we all had hoped to get some meaningful work in an actual metro market. *Arhhgggg!*

Significantly though, during these few months we had a couple of extended gigs; mainly at Sir Thomas Lounge in Racine, and also Cliff's Ridge up in Marquette, the ski lodge mentioned earlier. These gigs stabilized our finances but especially afforded Fred and me time to explore new musical turf: stuff for the real deal! Plus, with the place closed during the daytime we were able to rehearse on stage with all the gear in place.

It turns out Fred's dad, Harry, who was principal cellist for the Milwaukee Symphony, was a phenomenal musician; a career that included a long tenure with the Chicago Symphony. There was a program in Milwaukee headed up by a guy named Tom Truel who offered bands of a certain stature the chance to perform with the orchestra. Talk about mind-blowing excitement!

Obviously, we would need to provide original music, so Fred and I were doing cartwheels with excitement! What an opportunity! And to have the chance to perform with a world-class orchestra? Consequently, both of us rolled up our sleeves and got down to the business of creating real music for Matrix.

Oh yeah, I forgot to tell you; it was a freebie (non-paying performance) but we didn't care! Most groups would kill for such an opportunity and we relished the prospect. But then reality set in; this was no ordinary gig; this was the Milwaukee Symphony for godsake!

Pressure.

Well, faced with a deadline we had some serious humping to do. There was the need of an original conductor's score plus nine Matrix parts, and *arhgg*...add to that the need to provide thirty-two or more individual parts, one for each orchestra member (Note: each part was written by hand since this was before the days of Finale Music Notation!).

Yikes! We would need help. And ultimately, we would get it. But first and foremost, priority number one would be the score. That in itself was an enormous task and by far the most important.

Each page of an orchestral score starts at the top line with the piccolo, then flutes, oboes, clarinets, and so on down to the bottom line with double basses. In other words, an average of thirty-two individual lines of music to be written on each page for the entire orchestra.

Fred and I, both in our own ways, got after it, working diligently to not only do something worthy of the occasion, but to get all the parts done on time! Not that either of us needed more pressure, but hell, this was a big deal! And we wanted to make good for our Matrix brothers and, hopefully, not shank the opportunity or embarrass ourselves!

The two of us commiserated often and, at one point, Fred called me, sorely depressed. He wasn't sure whether he was up to the task of creating an original work with the pressure of a deadline.

I'm sure that some of his anxiety or misgivings came from the thought that his brilliant old man (and member of the orchestra) was looking over his shoulder. He was stuck. I'm sure it happens to any composer, author, poet, painter at some point...a classic case of "writer's block."

I did my best to calm his fears, encourage him, etc. but I remember saying to him, "For godsake, don't have a conniption fit over this!" I assured him he was more than capable and to just let his wonderful gifts take over.

# 11

As I said earlier, we needed help getting the tedious chore of part copying completed on time. *And* the parts had to be of professional quality! Remember, this was before computers and technology provided us with music notation software like Finale or Sibelius which are commonly used today. *This was the Milwaukee Symphony after all.*

So, when our scores were ready (properly hair-sprayed, yeah that's right: hair-sprayed to prevent the pencil copy from smudging) we turned them over to Keith Jackson, a former Lawrence University student, who was also known as 'Beer Hog.' (You can guess where that name came from!) He was a horn player/composer pal of the band and was happy to do it for us, thank God!

I, myself, have copied hundreds of parts and I assure you, it's a totally loathsome task! After the creative part has been completed, either the composer or a copyist has to start at the 'top' of the score and copy the individual part for each player. It's the composer's bane: the tiresome, unsatisfying grunt work of the process.

Beer Hog was a blessing! He was fast, accurate, and beautifully professional! We were glad to pay him, believe me.

Our next step was to meet with the conductor in his Milwaukee office. I was nervous as hell, never having been in this situation. So, white-knuckling in the chair opposite the maestro while he casually leafed through my score, "Ulysses" by name, I held my breath and waited for the ax to fall.

"Should be no problem at all," he offered with a hint of patronizing tone, or was I just super-hyper? Probably. '*Whew*,' I silently sighed, relieved that *that* was over. That evening after pizza with Fred's dad, Harry, he took us back to his apartment. He wanted to check for naïve errors which, of course, he was quick to point out thereby sparing us embarrassment at the rehearsal.

As I recall the dress rehearsal and performance were both on the same day the following week. From our point of view, Matrix was well-rehearsed and everyone seemed ready to go. So, let's do this thing. April 28, 1975, the much-anticipated day of our performance, finally arrived.

At the rehearsal, as I walked onto the stage with the orchestra busily warming up, the enormity of the moment hit me head-on like a semi! Talk about your deer in the headlights! My mind went *blank* and I think I felt like hurling. Any confidence I had previously enjoyed drained out of me like the flush of a toilet. Frankly, I was *scared!*

The agonizing wait was over. The conductor raised his baton for silence, then gave the downbeat for Fred's "Childhood's End." There was an intro by the orchestra and it all sounded totally foreign to me. Suddenly our Matrix guys hit these big chords which *I* was supposed to double. '*Geez! Are we there already?!*' I honestly felt I didn't belong here. It was a sickening feeling but, miraculously I found a modicum of composure and musical instinct kicked in.

I quickly found my place and we went through the piece nonstop. I must admit to being overwhelmed. Not by fear, but by the sheer beauty and power of Fred's score! It was truly a *wow* moment! 'Magnificent,' was all I could think (*tearfully*). I shall never forget the admiration for Fred that welled up in me to the point of tears! 'Bravo, dear friend!' What an unequivocal thrill!

Suddenly in my reverie, I heard the conductor say, "Ulysses!" Oh shit! All euphoria evaporated in a damned nanosecond! Sometimes reality can be a real pain in the ass, you know? "Ulysses" was a totally different musical animal, based on some 'twelve-tone techniques' that I was fond of using at times.

\* \* \* \* \*

*Twelve-tone composition uses the twelve chromatic pitches of our musical system and serializes them. This is referred to as the "tone row," which means putting them in a certain order which can then be repeated and kept intact. The sequence can be played upside-down (inversion) or backwards (retrograde) or retrograde-inversion but the integrity of the tone row is maintained throughout the piece.*

\* \* \* \* \*

The only thing I truly remember to this day was that "Ulysses" contained a ballad section which featured Dietch. His signature silky trombone sound, I remember, was absolutely beautiful!

After the rehearsal of "Ulysses," I asked if I might address the orchestra. Request granted, I spoke of the humbling honor we felt to be in their arena and how grateful we all were.

Then it was off to dinner before the big night.

# 12

I think I said 'dinner,' didn't I? No chance, Charlie! The way my insides were churning there was no way I could think of eating! I wandered out to the foyer of the auditorium and found Troll (Michael Bard) looking a bit lost, gazing out the window. He was expecting his girlfriend from Chicago and she was way overdue.

After casually chatting, he blurted out, "The hell with it! Want to catch a beer?" It was another two or three hours until showtime, and I jumped at the chance for a change of venue…and a beer or two.

Well, I distinctly remember having three beers by which time Troll and I were totally calmed. At least I was. No more fear, no more dread, no more self-doubt. Hmmm. To tell the truth, after the orchestra's couple of pieces (one of which was Richard Strauss's "Till Eulenspiegel") I was not only ready, but eager to get after it!

Following the orchestra's portion of the program, it was time to perform our original pieces with them. I took my place on stage at the keyboard, and was amazingly calm as I looked forward to our performance. The game had slowed down for me. I clearly remember playing enthusiastically and thoroughly enjoying the experience.

Looking out at the audience I recognized my close friend Barney and his wife. That's how clear everything was! The performance went very well, Fred's "Childhood's End" being the highlight for me. "Ulysses" went well too. And the audience ate it up! Of course, we had a number of well-wishers; even a group from Cliff's Ridge made the trip down for the show!

After the performance my friend Barney threw a party for Matrix and friends at the Milwaukee Inn, a fairly swank joint for the likes of us! Good old Barney! The beer flowed freely, deeply into the wee hours.

Man, it was one *hell of a* night!

# 13

The Milwaukee press gave us a fine review which, of course, made us feel pretty good about ourselves. But to me, the most significant dimension of the performance was our earnest effort to produce forward-looking, effective music and then…pull it off. Mission accomplished!

True, a long way to go, but a *big* step in the direction of our vision. We wanted to produce original stuff of high quality and make an impact on the jazz landscape.

It was Harry Sturm, a seasoned consummate pro, who gave me cause for hope and optimism. Not a man given to empty praise, he told me and Fred backstage after the gig: "What you're doing…(*choking up*) it's good. Keep on doing it…" I know his son was part of the equation, but the tiny tear in the corner of his eye said much, much more. I'll never forget that terse, emotional exchange backstage after our performance.

"Keep on doing it…" Thanks, Harry. We will; I promise.

# 14

It was shortly after the symphony date, through Michael Bard's Chicago connection, that we were introduced to the world of Sonart.

Sonart was a kind of production house/recording studio on the north side of Chicago. It was run by a guy named Chuck Lishon who was a thin little 'wannabe;' small in stature, large in self-worth. Through Troll's urging, Lishon offered to record what amounted to a demo for us, talking big plans: recording, touring, etc. I was in shock! It all seemed too good to be true.

Lishon assumed that, being the eldest member, I was the leader of the group. He sat me down in private, filling my head with promises and plans for the future…but recording?!? Wow! Exactly what we needed to do!

Soon we started laying down some tracks of our stuff in one of his recording studios (As I remember there were at least three in the facility). At this point in time, we still had a slew of gigs in Wisconsin, so between obligations we'd record some more tracks and then head north. This meant a bunch of trips to and from Chicago.

There were several friends living in the city which was a real blessing when it came to housing. Dietch was completing his master's at Northwestern University in Evanston and was maintaining an apartment in Chicago along with LU grad and close pal, Ken Orgel. Thanks to our friends' generosity, we saved a bundle on hotel costs. I just couldn't get over our good fortune!

No one minded sleeping on floors in a sleeping bag: a small price to pay for the good luck we were experiencing! So, this went on for a while, traveling back and forth between Wisconsin and Chicago.

Then one day Lishon called me into his office and explained to me that Sonart had already invested quite a bit in Matrix and suggested that a more legally binding arrangement would be mutually beneficial. As we knew, studio time was pretty expensive and, without laying out a penny, we had already logged a pretty substantial number of studio hours.

As a result of our meeting, I agreed to talk with everyone about a contract. Meanwhile, Lishon would have an attorney (it turned out to be his) draw something up. Fair enough, I thought. The band subsequently met in one of their vacant studios and I explained the situation as objectively as I could.

Then we voted. It was seven for, two against. The two negatives were me and Tony (Wagner), our drummer. Something about 'never sign anything without your own attorney's okay' stuck in my mind and so I voted 'nay.' Tony had other (perhaps intuitive) motives in his thumbs down.

But seven versus two meant it was a go. And truthfully, I was glad to be voted down, thinking of the recording and management potential. Besides, everyone at Sonart seemed cool, friendly, etc. What the hell…let's do it.

I clearly remember, on our next trip into Chicago, being invited into Chuck's attorney's office to go through each item of the contract with all nine members of the band present. Instead of baffling lawyer-speak, Chuck's smooth-talkin' boy took off his coat, rolled up his sleeves, and talked like 'one of the guys,' even sitting on the floor at one point.

It was almost like locker room fare spiced with vulgarities when he felt the need to keep us at ease; especially when there were certain dicey issues that may have been problematic to us…such things as royalties, percentages, controls, bookings, etc.

If there were questions or concerns, he would gloss over the point with something like, "Aw—that's just lawyer bullshit! Don't worry about it." I also remember not liking the guy. I hadn't connected any dots yet, but my instincts simply spoke quietly but firmly: I don't like this guy!

Oh well, the most important thing, or so I thought, was that we were heading in the direction that seemed right at the time.

And so, we signed.

In the weeks, even months that followed, I was expecting big things. You know, cool concerts, recording contracts, tours, etc. Instead, Sonart 'booked' a few private parties that Lishon set up for business associates and friends—of his.

One date in particular was at Mr. Kelly's, a very prestigious jazz venue. But, it wasn't for the public. It was an actual bar mitzvah! This was nothing more than a showcase for Lishon and his coterie of boot-licking friends!! What's worse, Lishon showed up in a leather shirt and pants with a leather Stetson hat, ala Clint Eastwood! As ludicrous as that was, he sat in on drums!

I don't have to tell you how pissed Tony was, and I sure as hell didn't blame him. And of course, Lishon totally sucked, though his cronies applauded enthusiastically. It was humiliating to say the least.

Damn, we were nothing but his plaything, to use as he pleased!

# 15

As I mentioned earlier, we had a number of Wisconsin gigs during our relationship with Sonart. What I didn't mention were the problems with Turd in his "managing." I think it may have been Tony that noticed some glaring improprieties with our finances.

Without going deeply into detail, as things unfolded it became obvious that we had to get rid of Mark. I mean, his writing of checks (he controlled our money) to pay for things we needed and then failing to sign them...big red flag! Well, during the delay of an unsigned check in the mail there was this money (that we had earned) dangling there for him to cherry pick. So...bye-bye, Turd.

I had no idea how much was ripped off. Nothing major, but it was a huge disappointment.

During one of our extended engagements at the Sir Thomas Lounge in Racine, Wisconsin (where we were quite popular, by the way), a somewhat 'unusual' event took place. Tex, our lead trumpet player, was celebrating a birthday so we decided to properly fete him. This resulted in a bit of overindulgence on our part prior to our evening's performance.

In plain English, we all got pretty soused.

Now Tom Fiorita, the owner of the club, really liked us owing to the fact that his joint was packed every night. He even threw a dinner for us. I think it was Troll who made the suggestion to close our first set with the usual fast-paced tune called "Matrix". However, there was a slight caveat: we would all switch instruments. (I 'played' soprano sax... Oh my god, *no!*)

Well, with the extraordinary collective alcohol level achieved before the gig, that seemed like a splendid idea! Everyone was trying to play a foreign instrument and the result was nothing but cacophony. To us, it was pretty hilarious, I can tell you! But Tom was not amused. He ended up docking us to the tune of two hundred bucks off our weekly wage.

You know what? It was worth it for the laughter that it elicited both from us and our fans, but especially us! Boys will sometimes be boys, don't you know...

Speaking of laughter, there are a fair share of happenings (humorous and otherwise) which I will refer to as 'Scattershots.' I use this term because putting these situations in accurate chronological order is nearly impossible owing to the fact that so many years have passed, and simple fading memory.

I had mentioned that when we needed to stay in Chicago for a few days, we relied on friends for a roof over our heads. On one particular occasion, Zap and I, sleeping bags in hand, wound up as the guests of Michael's girlfriend, Pam.

\* \* \* \* \*

*After a long day in Sonart's studio, the evening invited its customary wassail which meant copious amounts of beer consumed, also customary. When the need for sleep arrived, I chose a corner of what would be the living room, curled up in my bag, and drifted off to dreamland. Zap picked out Pam's $350 soft, poofy pillow as his headrest. He was on the other side of the room some twenty to twenty-five feet from me.*

*The only two times that I ever sleep walked in the past I did bad things, both times after more beer than I probably needed. Once, I pissed in the corner of our bedroom at our house, thinking I was positioned at the toilet. On another occasion, I locked myself out of my hotel room with nary a stitch on.*

*As far as bad things go, this occasion was no exception. At some point in the wee hours, still asleep, I headed across the twenty to twenty-five feet towards Zap. Pam's 'poofy' was my target.*

*Fortunately, Zap saw me coming and scrambled out of harm's way. When I arrived at my destination, I proceeded to empty my bladder on…you guessed it, the $350 pillow. Was this just plain dumb luck? Even in my stupor I had pretty good aim!*

\* \* \* \* \*

Needless to say, I was never invited back to 'Chez Pamela'.

# 16

It was the fall of 1975. The pop music scene was a swirl of names that meant little, at least to me: Springsteen, Alice Cooper, Elton John, Led Zeppelin, etc. And there were new movies: *Jaws* and *One Flew Over the Cuckoo's Nest*. A classic heavyweight battle took place in which Muhammad Ali beat Joe Frasier, known as the Thrilla in Manila…None of this activity affected any of us; we were too immersed in creating our own thing, I guess. Whatever.

The remainder of 1975 was spent working a variety of the usual Wisconsin haunts. We also had a handful of dates at a joint in Skokie, Illinois called Poor Richard's. Most of those gigs *we* had booked ourselves.

However, there was one gem that Sonart actually *did* book: we were to open for Weather Report at the Riverside Theater in Milwaukee on August 21, 1975. Talk about a night made in heaven—I mean Weather Report was our ultimate hero band and we were actually *opening* for them (I boldly shook Joe Zawinul's hand after the sound check)!

We were grateful for this gig, the only *quality* gig that they ever got us. We had become pretty disenchanted with Lishon's ego and Sonart in general.

I'm quite certain, however, that I speak for the entire band in saying that we were all personally grateful for this opportunity. I mean, come on…Joe Zawinul, Wayne Shorter, Jaco

Pastorius, and Chester Thompson! A pantheon of heroes. To be on the same stage with them was such an honor.

By then we had plenty of quality original music for a gig of this magnitude.

No covers that night! I remember we played a piece called "Justine," named after one of the books from *The Alexandria Quartet*. It was an arrangement which called for a fairly lengthy, rubato keyboard solo. I was feeling pretty good about what was unfolding musically, but I also had an odd sensation of a presence, or something.

Chimp, who was standing across the stage and had a perfect view behind me, told me afterwards that Zawinul was staring intently at me through a break in the curtain! A good thing I didn't know this, or I probably would have wet myself!

In any case, that evening was something I'll never forget. It was very telling that Lishon scoffed at the importance of Weather Report; he dismissed them saying, "These guys ain't much." Hell. He obviously didn't understand that much of our collective inspiration came from their highly evocative jazz/fusion style; they would remain a powerful influence throughout our story.

I guess the point is that our relationship with Sonart had deteriorated so badly that we had lost all faith in their ability to manage our career. With some of the material we had already recorded in their facility, we felt that many recording companies would jump at the opportunity to sign us just as Sonart had promised.

What the hell were they *doing*? It became glaringly apparent that they weren't capable of playing the game at the major league level.

Lishon was simply another small guy with a large ego; a minor league wannabe.

# 17

Our simmering anger boiled over with Sonart's total lack of substance and we tried to figure a way out of our contract. In short, we took the paperwork to an independent attorney for legal advice.

He read over the agreement and, after a brief pause, just shook his head. "You guys are in total bondage, for heaven's sake!" He had never seen such a lopsided contract in favor of management. "They can actually go after your families!"

Oh God! Talk about the Bumpkins and the Big City Slickers! A classic case of provincial naiveté on our part. The attorney's advice was simply to breach; his thinking was that no court of law would ever prosecute us for the complete unfairness of this document.

Well, that's what we did. We called them, gave notice, and walked.

Back home, I remember quite clearly receiving a phone call from Ed Rusk, Lishon's right-hand 'gofer' who I really liked. He was friendly, and actually seemed to care about us. At any rate, he called and pleaded with me to reconsider, saying they were closing in on a deal with RCA for a recording contract.

I was pretty certain that Lishon was listening in on another line and I remember telling Ed that I appreciated his efforts, but would never return. "You work for a snake, man!" I said. "I feel bad for you. Get the hell out of there while you can!" He (they?) rang off, and I thought, 'Good riddance!'

Not too long after our breach, we had a showcase gig at the NAMM (National Association of Music Merchants) at the Hilton Hotel on Michigan Avenue—downtown Chicago. Ironically, I think Sonart may have actually booked this job? Even though it was a freebie, it was a pretty big deal.

But so what? Bands would kill for such exposure! Thousands attended this huge expo with all the latest 'this and that' in the music industry, so we were pretty geeked up for the opportunity.

That night as we were announced and we were about to file up on stage, Ed Rusk stood there handing each of us a lawsuit subpoena for…(I'd never seen so many zeros!) *One million dollars! (phew)*

It was pretty obvious that this was Lishon's handiwork. Pretty good strategy when I thought about it later. Obviously, we weren't in the best psychological frame of mind for a scintillating performance and, I'm sure we were far less than our musical best. You can imagine the white-hot shock that floods through you when faced with a subpoena and the legal system (a terrifying animal!)

The worst thing I'd ever had from the law was an $18.00 speeding ticket. What the hell had we gotten ourselves into?

# 18

Along with our frustration at Sonart's ineptitude, we had issues of our own: our drummer, Tony, suddenly jumped ship, citing financial instability as well as, I guess, his disgust with management. We were able to cover most of our gigs, but it was a major pain in the ass especially having to find someone on such short notice.

We auditioned a couple Chicagoans and settled on one Vern Wennerstrom. He was a smart, likeable guy, but ultimately not what we were looking for in a drummer; his background was primarily rock-and-roll, lacking the versatility our 'good book' needed.

It was difficult letting him go because we all got along well enough in the few months that he was with us. But I believed our collective musical vision demanded a more diverse skill set than he could provide.

We ended up hiring a Wisconsin-born professional, Gary Miller. He had spent some time in Los Angeles and had a very impressive resume. Gary was a fine, all-around musician and an awfully nice guy to boot. At first, he played our stuff a bit too gently; that was fine for the quieter pieces, but for some of the more high-powered things...well, it wasn't quite happening.

Fred, in particular, was skeptical about Gary's approach. But finally, with a bit of behind the scenes prodding, Gary stepped up and kicked some serious ass! I'll never forget it!

We were playing Orphans, a north side Chicago jazz room. I'm pretty sure that it was on a hard ass-kicker, Fred's tune "Prana," that Gary took his playing to a level we hadn't yet heard!

When we finished the tune, Fred removed one of his shoes and inserted the toe into his mouth. Any questions? Problem solved!

Right time, right place, serendipity, etc. Once in a while, despite the unlikelihood, timing and destiny occasionally collide. By some cosmic stroke of chance, something happened that triggered a shift in our fortune; a veering off from the floundering direction of our career.

Somehow, almost unbelievably, one high-powered tune from the demo we'd made was played on a local Chicago jazz radio show. On his way to a tryst with a young lady, Dennis Justice, one of the Chicago office agents for Willard Alexander, was tuned to that station.

He heard Matrix playing one of our high-powered pieces (maybe Fred's "Earth and the Overlords") and in his words, '*totally* flipped!' He pulled off to the side of the road, called the lady he had planned to meet and said, "My dear…change of plans!"

After he learned the name of the band, he turned his car around and headed directly back to the office and phoned Willard himself with a *rave* review! After some inquiries, he found out that we would be at the aforementioned Poor Richard's. He picked up his lady friend, and went to hear us 'live.'

In his own words, "You guys [Matrix] were even more exciting in person!"

Dennis knew his way around the rarified air of the big boys. For years he had booked Willard's stable of heavyweights: Duke Ellington, Count Basie, Woody Herman, Stan Kenton, Thad & Mel, Buddy Rich and, ghost bands: Glenn Miller and Tommy Dorsey.

Ultimately, Dennis's enthusiasm for what he heard that night inspired him to convince Willard of our musical worth.

As it turns out, Zap went to high school in Rochester, Minnesota with Tom Cassidy, the head honcho in Willard's Chicago office. Hmm. Suffice it to say, something cosmic might be at work here.

# 19

Thank God for Dennis Justice! Hang on; I'll explain. After the breach, but prior to the lawsuit, we took things into our own hands. Roughly twelve years earlier a carpenter friend helped me build my dream house. It was west of Oshkosh with an alluring view of Lake Butte des Morts.

My recent divorce, and the subsequent sale of my home, left me single with at least fourteen thousand stashed in the bank. Having that money, I offered to finance our first recording date. Everyone agreed...with the provision that they pay me back over time. Fine with me. We needed a statement album, and this was the opportunity. The cash really meant a means to a much-needed end.

During the frequent Chicago dates, especially those at Poor Richard's, many of the Chicago-scene musical heavies showed up to check out this 'new kid on the block.' Among those who regularly came to hear us was a well-known trumpet player, Warren Kime, famous for some brass recordings he had made in the 1950s. He loved our brass-heavy instrumentation *and*, especially, all the original music we were presenting.

As memory serves, he urged us to record. Warren's enthusiasm for our recording potential and my previous offer to fund a recording date for the band set the wheels in motion. He had connections with, and recommended, Vern Castle's Studio in Lake Geneva, Wisconsin with engineer

Andy Waterman. Andy, a talented guy, would prove to be a valuable asset in our future recording career.

Then to my delight, Warren, with whom we had become friends, offered to produce it! He was the 'old pro' after all, and we all felt great about having his knowledge and guidance. So—funding, producer, recording studio, and engineer...It was a go; a match made in heaven!

Warren was such a blessing on so many levels. What the hell did *we* know? Studio rates were reasonable, close to Chicago for Warren, and best of all...in Wisconsin!

Chicago had left a bit of a sour taste in our collective mouths.

# 20

It was soon after the breach with Sonart that Dennis Justice's 'epiphany' at hearing Matrix, and his enthusiasm for what he had heard that fateful morning, ultimately paid off in spades for us. Dennis convinced *the* Willard Alexander to fly to Chicago and check us out in Lake Geneva! We were excited but well…scared shitless, so to speak.

Zap called Tom Cassidy (or maybe it was the other way around) and Tom assured him that Willard was "yeah, a giant, but *very* human; puts his pants on one leg at a time," etc. *To the chase!* Willard came to us, met us, heard us and, frankly…*loved* us. And *we* loved *him!*

Willard was far from intimidating in appearance. I would guess he was about five-foot-seven with thinning gray hair. Dressed in a conservative gray three-piece suit, the vest covering a bit of a spread, maybe late seventies or early eighties…a kind of reedy voice, he could have passed for a retired insurance salesman or some such.

You'd never know he was one of the most powerful, respected men in the music business. But Dennis would later share with us what a shrewd and sometimes mercurial employer he was. Dennis had, on occasion, been the recipient of Willard's wrath, and such moments were 'far from pretty' he would relate with a chuckle.

*But*, and this was huge, he wanted *us* in his stable. At that particular time, he had no cutting-edge, contemporary artist on his roster. Matrix fit his needs and when he made us an offer we were more than willing to say "Yes!"

I'm dead certain that when Sonart got wind of Willard's interest in us, their lawsuit, the outrageous million-dollar number, had something to do with their thinking. They saw Willard as the 'industry mogul' with deep pockets and were going to go for the big payoff.

As things unfolded, Willard informed us of a deal in the works, ironically with RCA Victor. But RCA wouldn't agree to any deal with an artist while they were under litigation.

'We'll see about that,' I can imagine Willard saying—for the very next thing he did was set up a head-to-head summit with Sonart with his own New York attorney. *Bring on the heavy artillery!*

I was present at this showdown and it was something to see! Willard's attorney, a man in his fifties, blue serge suit, stocky in build, pretty much took over the proceedings. He was stern, efficient, concise, and aggressive as he attacked Sonart's team. They were no match.

The bad news was that Willard's man set a figure of twenty grand for which we would ultimately be responsible. As Willard's attorney was bringing the meeting to a close it was downright pathetic to see one of Sonart's lawyers almost begging…$50,000, $40,000, $30,000, $20,000…

*Wham!* Willard's guy slammed his fist down. "I said *$20,000! That concludes our business here.*"

And that was that. The fact that they got *anything* galled the hell out of me. To Willard it was probably chump change but to *us*, that was a humongous sum.

I must confess I did *thoroughly* enjoy seeing Willard's attorney reduce the little pissants down to size. It was a profound relief (though at a price) to have, thanks to Willard, jettisoned the shackles of an incompetent and unethical managing company.

Now we belonged to Willard Alexander, the time-tested icon of jazz booking! And we were the only *truly* forward-looking, contemporary band on his roster!

This would lead to some interesting 'opening acts' for us.

# 21

The Kenwood Inn on the UW-Milwaukee campus was a regular weekend thing for us throughout the summer of 1976. One exception: no more covers! It was the 'good book' or nothing. And may the devil take the hindmost!

We kind of muddled along back in the trenches that summer. Summerfest was a pretty big deal in Milwaukee owing to the variety of national acts that were invited to perform. There were a number of different stages to accommodate various genres dominated by pop/rock/country groups. But, to their credit, Summerfest saw fit to feature jazz artists at the Miller Jazz Oasis.

A year earlier we had played a second-tier, off-the-beaten-track little venue for local rock bands. However, this year, the 'powers-that-be' running Summerfest recognized our worth and put us on the main stage for jazz artists.

Later that summer, we started working a west side Milwaukee night club called Giorgi's on a regular schedule. It was cool because, coupled with the regular Kenwood Inn gigs (also in Milwaukee), many local players of note came to hear us.

Also, being centered in Milwaukee, we would be able to hear some of the groups of reputation, especially Sweetbottom which featured Daryl Stuermer on guitar, Warren Wiegratz on alto sax, and Mike Murphy, their *killer* drummer!

Saxophonist John Kirchberger, from the group called September, came to hear us at the Kenwood Inn. I have to say that, in my mind, he was one of Milwaukee's premiere saxophone players. I immediately liked his gentle personality; he had proved to be a real musical force without an ounce of offensive ego that so often attends such gifted players.

My brief meeting with John brings us to an interesting contrast. Unfortunately, it seemed that Michael Bard was becoming a bit of a thorny problem. Issues with him began to simmer and ultimately boil over.

He began to increasingly embarrass our collective by showing up at venues assuming a 'leader' mentality, making 'professional' demands on the band directors and concert producers.

It was definitely *not* the Matrix way of doing things.

Michael's actions were rapidly becoming irritating and an embarrassment. I don't remember the straw that broke the proverbial camel's back, but a meeting was held and the decision was made to let him go.

As you might imagine this was painful on everyone, but especially on Dietch, who had taken over our finances after we let Mark Stenz go. The unfortunate issue with Michael would have to be dealt with later.

Excitement was brewing thanks to Dennis Justice who would become our unlikely 'angel.'

# 22

Bless you Dennis Justice for not only 'discovering' us, but especially for booking our first bona fide tour. And one hell of a tour at that, with the 'crown jewel' being an appearance at the Monterey Jazz Festival.

It's still beyond me how he sold Jimmy Lyons, the festival director, on an unknown, unrecorded (on any national label at least) nine-piece band of no-names. But he *did!*

A giddy atmosphere prevailed as we readied for the trip. But…oh yeah. How do we get from here to there? It so happened that Gary Miller had a van that seated eight or nine and he offered the use of it for obvious mileage compensation. Not exactly the most comfortable conveyance, but what the hell, we were young (well, *they* were!) and excited as all get out.

Come on! It's September 1976 and we were headed to California and the Monterey Jazz Festival!

If memory serves, Chimp's dad (owner of Pat Long Chevrolet) provided a high cube equipment truck for our instruments, gear, and luggage. I believe we rented the truck that later became nicknamed 'Moon Unit.'

So we were off and running and don't think we minded the cramped quarters of Gary's van that much. Somehow, we managed the logistics of travel, despite less than optimum comfort.

Monterey Jazz Festival, of course, had their own sound company but for all other dates before and after, we needed a sound man. How we 'acquired' Joe Ott, I can't really recall. A sweet guy, but totally unqualified for such a gig. We would worry about that later.

And what the hell…we were playing Monterey!

Our first date of the tour was in Santa Rosa, California at Santa Rosa Junior College. As the date was September 17, 1976, we encountered no problems getting through the mountain pass in terms of snow and the need for chains.

Our first actual gig was a noon concert at an outdoor site on campus. Santa Rosa Junior College was a lovely little venue. It was very casual with students strolling past, or just hanging out. We enjoyed our forty-minute program to a modestly positive response.

I think some of the unmarried guys in the band were especially taken with the suntanned, healthy-looking (mostly blonde) co-eds wandering by. At the union cafeteria, Dietch remembers Fred going absolutely crazy over his food order: a Monterey Jack, avocado, and sprout sandwich. He was a strict vegetarian, so this was a big deal for him!

As part of our agreement, we were asked to do an improvisation clinic later in the afternoon. Improv was pretty much my bailiwick, so I remember basically running it. I recall being 'sort of challenged' by the jazz director and was able to extricate myself from what seemed to be a corner I'd painted myself into. No biggie.

That evening the concert went very well, and we left Santa Rosa feeling pretty good having been very well-received.

Next…Monterey. Bring it on!

# 23

Sunday, September 19, 1976, was a day none of us would ever forget. Sometimes you just get lucky. Maybe it was written in the stars. But whatever the reason, this year's three-day festival offered mostly conventional, straight-ahead groups.

The most forward-looking presentation I remember was Jack DeJohnette's percussion ensemble. So, up until Sunday evening when we were slated to perform, we heard (as did the audience) pretty much middle-of-the-road stuff. Oh, *great* stuff—don't get me wrong. But the door seemed to be open for us; all we had to do was charge through it.

Understandably, the magnitude of the event, the Monterey Jazz Festival (our first major gig under Willard's wing) put a little edge on our collective psyche or mine at least. I mean, come on…this was one of the premier jazz events in the country! And here we were, a bunch of midwestern guys with no name recognition, no record deal, and despite a little nervousness, ready to get after it.

I'll never forget the sound check before the gates opened to the public. We were scheduled to open the Sunday night concert. During our warm-up on stage, we played maybe sixteen bars of "Catalpa Complex" before the crowd queued up outside started hootin' and hollerin'. It was as though they were primed and ready for something new, fresh, and exciting! Well, I'm pretty damned sure we answered the call.

Naturally we played a set from our 'good book.' Although we all believed in what we were doing, the music itself had never been validated by a huge, knowledgeable audience of this size and sophistication. Attendance, by the way, was close to seven thousand! Any doubts about audience response were soon dispelled; they seemed to love everything we threw at them. And we were playing great!

I remember feeling a surge of, I guess it was pride, as I stepped to the mic to announce whatever the next piece was. By God, we were being validated in spades! The audience was hearing sounds that they'd never been exposed to and were loving it (as I relate this I'm welling up with emotion)! We were actually *doing* it! The dream; the vision. It was happening!

But the kicker was our closing piece, Fred's "Childhood's End," inspired by the Arthur C. Clark book. It was the scaled-down version of the piece that we had premiered with the Milwaukee Symphony Orchestra. Fred had scored a synthesized ascending crescendo to accompany the dramatic finish as it was coming to its kick-ass conclusion.

As if orchestrated by God himself, a huge jet roared over the facility in perfect sync with the synthesizer! And with the last rapid, virtuosic, precisely executed passage and 'stinger,' the crowd went bonkers, leaping to their feet in thunderous approval!

Honest to God, I'd never experienced anything like it! We were all kind of stunned, never having gone through anything this powerful. I didn't know whether to laugh or cry.

But I did know one thing: Matrix, this bunch of idealistic dreamers, was *something special.*

# 24

After acknowledging the overwhelming response to our performance, we exited the stage and were greeted by several guys (four, I think) with microphones. They shoved them at us asking excitedly, "Where are you guys from?" "Have you been recorded?" "How come we haven't heard of you before?" etc. They were from various West Coast jazz radio stations, having broadcast us *live* during our performance. Up and down the coast the band Matrix became the buzz!

We've all heard of Hollywood-scripted overnight sensations, and that's sort of what happened I guess, at least on the West Coast. But the coolest thing for me, at least, was that my wife, Traf (Linda), had flown out from Wisconsin to join up with us and was able to witness this magical moment first-hand! The fact that a jet flying overhead right when it did, which added to the climax of the piece, was as thrilling to her as it was to us.

*And*, if *that* wasn't enough, it was September 19, 1976, Zap's birthday!

The icing on the cake for this momentous occasion was that my dear friend and Matrix supporter, Barney, had given me an envelope with instructions to open *after* our Monterey performance. After we were packed up and ready to go, I opened it. Inside was a beautiful note of encouragement and fifty dollars to use in celebration.

So naturally, our first stop as we were leaving Monterey, was to buy fifty dollars' worth of the Mexican beer, Dos Equis. We were scheduled to give a clinic and concert the next day at the College of the Siskiyous in Weed, California. But *that* night belonged to us!

So, when we arrived at our lodging, we had one helluva party. We certainly honored Barney's request in grand style, toasting him again and again as seemed appropriate. And frankly, who could blame us?

It turned out to be one of two career-changing events on this, our first tour.

# 25

I guess you could say we were flying pretty high after our Monterey triumph. The ensuing gigs (with a clinic/concert at College of the Siskiyous, and performances at University of Nevada, Reno and Los Banos High School in Los Banos, California) were performed with a new dimension of confidence owing to our success at Monterey. It seemed to validate what we were doing in a profound way.

Next, we cruised into Las Vegas to open for, if memory serves me, Jimmy Witherspoon at the Las Vegas Jazz Society. Our host for the appearance was Monk Montgomery, renowned pioneer of electric bass in the jazz landscape, and president/founder of the society. This gentle, soft-spoken man was so gracious, so welcoming, and so humble for a name of his magnitude. A beautiful man in every sense of the word.

As it turned out, for one reason or another, the headliner for the concert couldn't get out of Los Angeles and had to cancel. As a result, Monk approached us to ask if we would consider doing a second set to cover the situation. We gladly accepted the invitation.

Before we actually played, Monk went out on stage announcing the change in the program and that Matrix would perform a second set. Monk then offered the caveat that he would refund anyone's money who was disappointed in the regrettable circumstance.

Once again, we went out and played our hearts out for this packed house—as much for Monk—as for the paying audience. I guess we did okay because not only did we get a standing ovation, but not one fan asked for their money back.

I'll never forget Monk's response after the gig. With tears in his eyes, he thanked us with such quiet warmth that I'm feeling emotional as I write this. He also took down all our names and addresses, officially naming us honorary members of the society which meant that we would each be receiving the Las Vegas Jazz Society's monthly newsletter.

I remember getting the newsletter in the form of a small paper for years until his demise, at which time the society either dissolved, or perhaps changed such policy. What a profound lesson in humility by this man's example. He certainly made *my* personal Hall of Fame.

Maybe this wasn't *career*-changing, but seeing him as a human being was definitely *life*-changing.

Onward to Redondo Beach, California, September 28–October 3, 1976, and a week at Howard Rumsey's Concerts by the Sea, one of the more prestigious jazz venues on the West Coast. Man, oh man, life under the Willard umbrella (and Dennis Justice, of course!) was pretty damned cool!

I mean, come on: our very first tour and we play Monterey Jazz Festival, Las Vegas Jazz Society, and now Concerts by the Sea!? When I think back on all those shit gigs early on, doing covers of pop music, etc…every gig on this junket was so classy. And the bread was so much better as well.

Descending the stairwell at Concerts by the Sea to set up our gear in the club's performance area, we were blown away to see Leonard Feather's *glowing* review from our performance at the Monterey Jazz Festival. I had never seen this review. There it was in five-inch letters adorning the walls for all to see.

So, this is what the high end is all about?! For a bunch of no-name guys out of Wisconsin, this was pretty heady stuff, believe me!

The five nights at Concerts by the Sea were a total gas! Howard himself would bring us on over the PA and, at the end of our last tune, he would say something like, "Beautiful set, guys! Aren't these fellas something special?" Which, of course, elicited more enthusiastic applause.

To our surprise, probably due to the buzz we created at Monterey, the aforementioned Leonard Feather showed up, the renowned critic for *DownBeat* and the *Los Angeles Times*.

We had plenty of high-powered things in our book. One piece that I specifically remember playing was "Nessim," an exotic kind of Egyptian mood piece with a repetitive bass figure, evocative, and somewhat haunting. It had four-part vocal backgrounds with extremely difficult chromatic harmonies that Tex, Zap, Fred, and Dietch easily pulled off.

It's still, after all these years, one of my favorite pieces… but hardly what you might expect from a band that (given the opportunity) could peel the paint off a back wall!

Obviously taken with the uniqueness of our stuff, Mr. Feather wrote yet another beautiful article, I mean a *stunning* review, in the *Los Angeles Times*. One phrase will always stand out in my memory:

*"…the sound of surprise is never more than seconds away…"*

It was a beautiful testament to the musical goals to which we all aspired. And *this*, by Leonard Feather, after all! His assessment was, in fact, career changing.

Not only were we well-received but several iconic jazz luminaries showed up at Concerts by the Sea to check us out like…Lew Tabackin, Toshiko, Hampton Hawes, for example. Also, a couple of guys I knew from my term in the Army reached out. One Jerry Grant, fine saxophone player, *actually came* to the gig. Jackie Wilson, another friend and one hell of a jazz pianist, initiated a lengthy phone call to catch up since our time in the Army. Thank you, Leonard Feather.

This was what working with Willard Alexander was all about. What a tour! We could handle this! Work the hell out of us!

I might add, "Be careful what you wish for…"

# 26

We finished this memorable tour on October 9 in Yuma, Arizona and headed home. To tell you the truth, returning to the local scene seemed anticlimactic after all the 'glamor gigs' of that month. From the beginning of September through the middle of October we were back in the comfort of our local environs.

Through Willard, we did one noteworthy opening for the Basie Band in Wausau, Wisconsin which kept the inner fires glowing. A series of the usual haunts, working the Kenwood Inn, Josef's, Poor Richard's, and a scattering of local 'throwaways,' kept us playing plus it provided the opportunity to create new material.

Unfortunately, the heady glow of what we had enjoyed from the previous month's prestigious gigs fell pretty much on deaf ears of the local musicians. They had no clue as to what we had accomplished. Ah yes; *reality*…Wisconsin and Illinois, for that matter, are a long way from California.

We all know the phrase, 'A prophet doesn't succeed in his own hometown,' or some such. 'Hey! We just blew everyone away at the Monterey Jazz Festival, Concerts by the Sea, etc.…' An indifferent '*Uh-huh*' was pretty much the local response. Man! What do we have to do to earn the well-deserved respect we felt we should be getting? Ah, yes…*reality*…

'Where are your recordings?' the general public seemed to ask with more than a hint of skepticism. These silent questions screamed at me: 'Have you played Birdland? Slug's? The Blue Note?' In all honesty I was pissed. So what? We kept playing the usual venues.

As I'd mentioned earlier, there were issues concerning Michael's behavior. It was something we needed to deal with, *and soon*. There were so many things I liked about Michael, but he was exhibiting a 'leader-mentality' that was offensive to the rest of us, and this was definitely not the 'Matrix way'…No *one* person ever assumed full leadership. This was a collective.

Eventually there was a pretty ugly severance with Michael. It was especially difficult for Dietch, our treasurer, who still lived in Chicago and had the unpleasant task of dealing with Michael's *very* irate grandmother.

We ended up paying through the nose for things that Michael demanded like rehearsal time (geez, are you kidding?), instrument upkeep, emotional suffering…you get the idea.

Because of the enormous debt we had previously incurred (to wit: Willard, as well as his lawyer, flights for both round trips, etc)…all of this put us deeply in the red, a hole we never completely crawled out of.

While we were in California on the aforementioned tour, Fred had actually called John Kirchberger and Murph and hinted at the possibility of openings in Matrix. Fred and Chimp, who knew both Kirch and Murph, also had heard that the bands they currently played in were going through some changes. If, and when, these two fabulous players became available, we were all thrilled at the prospect of hiring them should they find our offer appealing.

And then there was a problem with Gary Miller over some issues with his van. It was some personal stuff that I wasn't privy to, or simply can't recall. But aside from that, I do remember that Gary was not quite what we were looking for musically. He was a fine musician but lacked the contemporary drive that we needed in a drummer.

I still remember how painful it was giving Gary the news and, to his credit (though somewhat bitter) was a gentleman about being let go. I will always admire his ultimate professionalism.

Knowing that Michael and Gary would soon be leaving, both the saxophone and drum slots needed to be filled, so Fred initiated offers to Kirch and Murph. The Willard Alexander Agency was now currently booking the band and Willard *himself* was closing in on a recording deal with RCA Victor to release our already existing album (vinyl, of course).

I'm sure this prospect certainly 'sweetened' the deal. We now had a brilliant saxophone soloist (who could double on flute and soprano as well) and a driving force in the rhythm section that excited us all.

The 'engine' was now fired up and ready to go!

# 27

In Fred's own words, "When Murph and Kirch joined, we became contemporary!" We all fully embraced the two new guys (polar opposites as personalities) and could they *play!*

Murph (who later was nick-named 'Miff Murk-ee') was an aggressive, hard-charging, serious ass-kicking drummer that could curl your hair should the music call for it. But he also possessed a wonderful sensitive side to handle our gentler pieces. He read music well and absorbed things quickly, so it didn't take him long to learn our ever-expanding book of original stuff.

He never flaunted his Irish-ness but he knew what to do with a glass in his hand! And yes…he had a bit of a temper, but what an incredible sense of humor he possessed; a total bonus on long road trips!

Kirch, one of the gentlest souls I've ever known, a non-preachy devout Christian, was a musical titan! He was soft-spoken and humble yet, when he picked up the tenor, had this aggressive, full-bodied sound playing virtuosic solos that dazzled listeners, especially his bandmates!

He also, by the way, authored some extremely subtle, hilarious pranks which still, after all these years, make me smile. Humor is such a tonic on lengthy road trips and both these guys provided plenty in that department. Moreover, their musical contributions certainly kicked us up a notch as a band.

* * * * *

*John Kirchberger, our brilliant saxophone/flute player, is a devout Christian, a gentle soul, soft-spoken, with a 'wicked' sense of humor. If you happened to sit next to him on a long trip you were more than likely to become a 'victim' of what came to be known as "GPS." Not to be confused with the current satellite guidance gizmo.*

*Here's how it worked: He was a great conversational companion which was helpful on long rides. His exceptional intellect made for fascinating, engaging conversation. It was easy to get caught up in whatever the topic.*

*His personal warmth could easily get an unsuspecting person fully absorbed, unaware of the slightest elbow pressure in one's side. Perhaps over a ten-to-fifteen-minute span, with utmost skill and discipline, he would ever-so-gradually increase the pressure by the tiniest of increments. Interest in the conversational exchange made one oblivious to the subtle trap he had laid.*

*By the time the pressure of his elbow obviously became severe, you realized you'd 'been had.' Kirch would explode with little bursts of laughter! Of course, the victim would also break up, knowing he'd been duped by a superior prankster.*

*In our world, GPS didn't mean Global Positioning System… It stood for 'Gradual Pressure Syndrome.' It remains one of the subtlest, most hilarious jokes I've been the fool of…and lived to tell about!*

* * * * *

Much was changing in our total makeup during the month or so of regional (non-Willard) gigs: Giorgi's, Josef's, Fire Alarm, The Dilemma, Kenwood Inn, etc. With another tour coming up, there were serious needs to be addressed: sound man, sound system, transportation vehicle and, oh yeah…roadies: guys to set up and tear down our gear before and after gigs.

Let's start with the sound man. Zap was close friends with Peter Butler, a brilliant sound guy who he'd played with in a high school rock band called Therica. Peter played bass in the band and owned some state-of-the-art sound equipment. *And* he knew how to use it!

Though his name was Peter, everyone called him 'Herb.' Through Zap's urging, he agreed to come on board and a couple of serious issues were resolved: sound man and sound system. In time we would discover what a wizard this guy was with the 'knobs' (dials on the soundboard).

Obviously with Gary gone, we were without a suitable vehicle to transport nine guys around the country *plus* a sound man and, hopefully, a roadie or two. Enter Chimp, or specifically, Chimp's dad.

His father owned a large automotive company in the Milwaukee burbs, 'Pat Long Chevrolet.' His company dealt with all the Chevy line of cars, trucks, RV's, and motor-homes. Well, to our everlasting good luck, Mr. Pietrangelo (Pat Long) offered us a pretty high-end thirty-two-foot motorhome, and thanks to our somewhat iffy (inconsistent) income, a liberal leasing plan as well.

I have already mentioned his earlier generosity concerning the high cube equipment truck (also leased) so Mr. Pietrangelo was, indeed, a godsend. Of course, if his son (an incredible feature in the band) was going to traipse around the country, Mr. Pietrangelo wanted him (and the rest of us, presumably) to travel in some comfort.

What tremendously good fortune to have access to a dealership of this size and scope at our fingertips.

\* \* \* \* \*

*Early on in the motorhome, it was decided to have Fred make his heralded spaghetti. There was, after all, a gas stove as a feature on the Georgi Boy (its trade name). Hell of an idea, which got enthusiastic approval from all of us. Hell of an idea, that is, when the motorhome was stationary…not wheeling down the interstate at 65 mph!*

*The first bump in the road sent a cup or so of near-boiling water onto the tennis-shoed foot of Chimp. He started screaming as if he were being burned at the stake; such howling as I'd never heard issued forth! I'm sure it didn't feel good having scalding water hitting one's foot…but, well let's just say his threshold for pain may have been a bit on the low side.*

*And frankly, it wasn't the smartest idea to try and cook while speeding down the highway. So big 'bad on all of us' for not recognizing the folly of our thinking—or lack of it.*

*An addendum to the scalded foot episode:*

*I accompanied Chimp to the emergency room to have his foot tended. Dietch and Fred remained in the motorhome while others scattered for various reasons. Both of them noticed Chimp's soggy sock on the floor. One of them, I'm sure, in a melodramatic delivery intoned, "The fatal sock!" Both of them howled with laughter.*

*Chimp, who was very good at getting out of work, milked his accidental injury to avoid the grunt work of setting up and tearing down the equipment (He often complained about some mythical 'sciatica' for the same reason as I recall).*

\* \* \* \* \*

After this infamous episode someone got to a toy store (I suspect it was Lauben) and found a black-colored plastic chimpanzee. Up behind the driver there was a runner with a curtain that could be closed for night driving separating the driver from lights in the main passenger area.

With the curtain opened and secured with a Velcro strap, there was the entire runner free and clear. Someone cleverly affixed a white piece of cloth around one foot of the toy chimpanzee and fastened it to the curtain track. So, every time the motorhome made a turn, the toy 'chimp' would slide in the opposite direction; an hilarious reminder of our stupidity and, of course, the melodramatic shrieks of our beloved Chimp.

Oh yeah, we needed someone to help with the heavy lifting.

Again, it was Zap to the rescue. At the time he was married to Diane Lautenschlager, or D.K. as everyone called her. Very hip jazz advocate. It turns out that one of her brothers, Doug, wasn't doing much at the time so, I guess he somewhat jumped at the chance to 'get out of Dodge' and do an adventure.

I'm a bit hazy on detail here, but Doug and Herb seemed to hit it off pretty quickly as we plodded through our regional gigs. I do remember as it turns out, with all the shit we had to schlep for our shows, Doug and Herb were a welcome addition in many ways. When our performances were finished, we all took turns signing off on stage by introducing everybody including Herb and Doug.

Well, on one particular closing, Kirch, fairly new to the band, drew the short straw. And as he was flawlessly running through the band members, he got to Herb, then when he got to Doug…*long pause*…(he couldn't remember Lautenschlager) finished up with "our road assistant…Lauben." We all cracked up but of course, the name 'Lauben' stuck. And to this day we all still call him that.

I should add that, through our many adventures, Lauben became, and remains, beloved.

# 28

Enter 1977. Jimmy Carter became the new president and *Star Wars* opened in cinemas. In the life of Matrix, it was new music, new players, new sound man, etc. Everything hunky-dory right? Maybe not.

Before we headed out of Wisconsin, I failed to mention that on April 30, after a long rehearsal at Josef's in Appleton, we had a meeting requested by Fred. No big deal. Normally we had a lot of "think-tanking" after practicing.

None of us were ready for the bombshell about to hit us: with deep regret, Fred announced that though he would do the tour, he was giving notice that he could no longer commit to the dream.

Of all things, after Fred's emotional presentation, bassist Randal Fird also gave the same kind of notice. What the hell! From out of the blue, lightning had struck twice! The shock was palpable; it would be more accurate to say we were stunned. Nobody said a word for a bit, each of us trying to process what just went down.

In Fred's case, I think there was some level of understanding: I think he had an eye on a teaching position. And if anyone was a born educator, it was *him*. Not only was he an unbelievably creative and superb musician, but he also possessed a very lovable, all-American personality. *Everyone* admired and looked up to him! How do we replace a charismatic influence like Fred?

And then there was Randal, a quiet, gentle giant who had supplied us with a rock-solid foundation. His soloing was totally unique: beautiful, lyrical, sensitive, and wonderfully imaginative. How in the hell do we survive this double hit?

The obvious musical absence was *one* thing, but emotionally…we *loved* these two guys! There is no appropriate cliché to cover this situation. We all just gritted our teeth and got on with it. We had a tour to do, and that was that.

And what a tour it was! No time to fret over our considerable troubles.

# 29

"Breaker 1-9, Breaker 1-9, do you copy?" We now had new CB radio communication devices connecting our vehicles. Starship was the 'handle' for the beautiful thirty-two-foot motorhome and the equipment truck was dubbed Moon Unit.

So here we were, on the road, starting another tour under Willard's wing, and riding in style! This was something we could definitely live with.

Our first stop, January 13-14, 1977, was a two-day festival in Sacramento, California. We stayed in the home of the Sacramento City College jazz director *for free*. It was quite an expansive, lavish pad, including a big indoor pool. The owner wasn't there, so we had free run of the place.

Our gig included a concert plus two days of judging combos and big bands. The first day Dietch, Murph, and I were at the judge's table. It was a long day of combos, most of which were predictably in need of experience/growth. However, a few were quite impressive.

The most memorable event of our day was not a musical moment and had nothing to do with judging (*chuckle*). It was a brown paper bag lunch that had been left on the judge's table with the name 'Keith Farley' written on it.

As our day concluded, young Mr. Farley's brown bag remained unclaimed. Inside the bag (we *had* to look) Murph discovered a baloney sandwich, an apple, and a Snickers bar.

Murph instantly went into comedic mode. In a high-pitched nasal voice he delivered:

"Uh, Mrs. Farley, we have your son's baloney sandwich here; uh, could you let him know…"

He spiraled that into a spate of hilarious re-enactments that had Dietch and me in stitches. It was the perfect antidote to a long day of judging. In the coming weeks, Keith Farley became the subject for a series of goofy announcements:

"Attention: Keith Farley! We are in Topeka and we want you to know we have your lunch! It's beginning to smell funny…"

"…and by the way, I ate the Snickers bar." etc., etc., etc.

On one of our stops in Nevada, we were scheduled to play an afternoon concert at the University of Nevada-Las Vegas. Ray Charles was playing at one of the big hotels and several musicians from his band came to check us out.

After our performance, Ray's guys introduced themselves along with enthusiastic compliments for our program. After a bit of social shoptalk one of them offered, "Anyone interested in tickets for Ray's show that evening, just come a little early through the big double doors into the kitchen. I'll get you passes."

"Beautiful," I thought. "I love Ray Charles!"

\* \* \* \* \*

*As it turns out, Murph and I were the only ones to take him up on the offer. It was probably forty-five minutes before the show when we arrived. We went through the kitchen, surprised to find no one there. So we made our way to what turned out to be the left side of the stage.*

*There was a large black curtain (called 'legs' in theater par-lance) maybe ten feet high that shielded audiences from backstage activities. In this particular leg, there was a wrap-around fold whose function escaped me. Murph and I were a bit uneasy as our presence could be construed as trespassing.*

*Suddenly, the big double doors at the kitchen entrance banged open and two big, beefy guys came stomping in. Bouncers! Murph and I instinctively ducked out of sight into the wrap-around fold I had mentioned. These guys looked serious.*

*Damn! There aren't any musicians here yet and I didn't remember any names of the band members! Again, damn! If we're caught here, we're gonna get our asses kicked! Here we are: can't move, can't talk, can't hardly breathe!*

*Finally, players start filing in and begin their pre-show war-mups. But we're stuck in the fold of this curtain.*

*Soon some perfumey women start vocalizing: The Raylettes, backup singers for Ray. And they're not ten feet away! Imagine the fun should we be discovered!*

*I mean, come on…two male 'trespassers' in the presence of scantily clad 'defenseless' Black ladies! We could hear everything they said, none of which I can repeat…But that's how close they were to us.*

*The old sphincters had to work overtime to put a check on the lower tract! Finally, the damned show actually started and miraculously we weren't discovered!*

*We ended up hidden for the whole show. Strangely, our lis-tening was less than satisfying even though we were maybe two feet from the organist. Because of our proximity we couldn't hear any balance from the band.*

*One section would be louder than another and Ray sounded like he was off in another room. Frankly, we didn't give a damn.*

*When the show was over it was the same routine: don't move a muscle! We had to wait a good twenty minutes before the backstage area finally cleared.*

*With an enormous sense of relief, we beat a hasty retreat.*

\* \* \* \* \*

After our, let's say unusual 'entertainment' for the evening, Murph and I headed back toward our motel. To me, Las Vegas at night is a wasteful vulgarity of electric power; an embarrassing display of glitzy overkill. But the street leading to our motel, once a few blocks from the downtown area, had to be the dimmest-lit street in town; perhaps a normal streetlight every fifty yards.

\* \* \* \* \*

*Maybe twenty paces in front of us was an elderly couple in evening clothes. Murph and I were jabbering away, laughing at our little caper, when we noticed a sudden flash. No big deal. The couple ahead of us had just taken a photo.*

*When we arrived at the point of the flash, we saw the subject: a heart-wrenching elderly Black man seated in the grass... begging. We hustled past the poor guy looking straight ahead.*

*I noticed the woman nonchalantly toss something onto the grass bordering the sidewalk. When we got to the spot of the 'toss' I picked up a Polaroid photograph. It was a close-up of the poor, pathetic beggar, discarded like a piece of trash. Murph and I were stunned!*

*There was such humiliation and anguish in this unfortunate man's eyes! He was very dark-skinned, but the flash glazed his features with a subtle bluish cast.*

*I still have an indelible image of that man's face after all these years! I hung onto the photograph. We were both pretty silent the rest of the way back.*

*   *   *   *   *

The only reason I've gone to such lengths to tell of this is as follows: it led to me composing one of our most unique pieces for the album *Harvest*, released on the label Pablo Today. The composition has no improvisation. It is simply called "Blue Black." In it, I tried to capture the anguish written on that poor guy's face.

You be the judge: I think I got it.

# 30

Back to California. After Sacramento it was on to Santa Rosa for a return engagement at Santa Rosa Junior College on January 15, 1977. Again, we enjoyed a wonderful response, especially with our new powerhouse players, Kirch and Murph. Before heading on to Merced College, we had a short break.

We were able to spend a couple of nights at a motel in redwood country, Guerneville, California. It was a welcome recreational time: throwing the football around, frisbee tossing, or meandering amongst the ancient redwood trees. *Totally* magical!

After Merced College it was then on to Cerro Coso Community College in Ridgecrest, California. I remember these 'virgin' audiences loved the unique, programmatic nature of much of our repertoire. I think they were taken with our unique way of using voices as color background.

Sometimes I would score Zap to 'vocally double' a soprano sax part or say, trumpet passage using Harmon mute. This created a very unique sound. It all seemed to be working well for audiences judging by the feedback from listeners after our concerts.

Next was a six-nighter at the Playboy Club in Century City in downtown Los Angeles January 24–29, 1977. There was this comedienne, Lotus Weinstock, who opened for us each night. Her 'shtick' got a little old by the end of the week. I mean, the same not-great jokes night after night...*sigh*.

And, unfortunately, the crowds were skimpy because people were staying at home to watch the new compelling TV series, *Roots*.

What *was* memorable about the week was Willard showing up with the legendary band leader, Artie Shaw! Meeting him was a real thrill. He was very articulate and extremely complimentary of our music. So, in the confidence department, we were feeling pretty good about ourselves.

What we were doing...if it was well-received by the likes of Mr. Shaw...well, we could tell we were on the right track.

However, a closer look at the itinerary brought us back to earth in a heartbeat. To wit: we finished the gig approximately twelve to one o'clock in the morning on Saturday night in downtown Los Angeles and were scheduled to open at Joe Rico's Airliner Motel on—*gulp*—Tuesday in Miami, Florida!

Are you flippin' kidding? What were they thinking back there in the Chicago office? Probably laughing their collective asses off! I mean, that's about as far as you can go in the forty-eight continental states, for God's sake!

There were several of us that shared the driving responsibilities but, remember we had *two* vehicles! So...after some seventy hours on the road with gas and food—pit-stops— we arrived Tuesday around six-thirty a.m. at the Airliner Motel. Mr. Rico took one look at this bleary-eyed group and mercifully canceled our opening night.

Grateful would be an understatement; we were fried to the max.

# 31

Once fully rested, everything about the gig was cool; no travel (*Amen!*), same bed, time to rehearse with nice, knowledgeable crowds (many from University of Miami jazz students and faculty) who seemed to be into what we were doing.

Plus, some of the local 'heavies' showed up. For example, Ira Sullivan, legendary Chicago icon (tenor/trumpet) and The Crusaders' keyboard player, Joe Sample. Their positive feedback was reassuring.

But a bigger plus was about to happen. We let it be known that the bass trombone chair, as well as the bass guitar position, were opening. A bass trombonist from the University of Miami contacted us expressing an interest, so an audition was set up at the club.

I remember *so* clearly what happened when Brad McDougall showed up. He took his horn out of the case, put it together, and started to do a preliminary warm-up. Fred heard his tone, turned to Dietch, and sort of under his breath I heard him say, "If he can read, he's the one!"

Well, he *could* read! We went through a couple of things and he was flawless. It was a slam dunk situation. Almost as important as his fine musicianship, his personality was totally cool, the kind of guy you immediately liked. *Plus*, he was a Midwestern boy, brought up on a farm in northern Illinois. Not quite Wisconsin, but close enough.

With Fred's full approval, we all welcomed him, confident that he was the right guy for the job. And he was just that...*in spades!* Talk about your perfect fit! Did we just get lucky, or was this one written in the stars? I think maybe, a little bit of both.

As I recall, Fred did finish this tour because Brad had some loose ends to tie up; he'd join us later.

# 32

The next stop was another *week-long* gig (February 14-20) in Atlanta. The Harlequin Dinner Theatre was the venue. Talk about unique! The physical layout was fashioned after a Shakespearean theater-in-the-round—large, mahogany-colored wooden beams and benches everywhere. Extremely cool!

Our first night we played a late set after—guess who—? The Duke Ellington Orchestra! The band was fronted by Duke's son, Mercer and, to tell the truth, it was a bit disappointing. Most of the legendary guys: Johnny Hodges, Harry Carney, Lawrence Brown and, of course, Duke himself, were already gone.

I won't say the band was just going through the motions, but frankly, some of us thought they were. No matter; we got to see and meet some of the players. Plus, we could always brag about it: *the* "Duke Ellington Orchestra" opened for Matrix in Atlanta!

Funny, laughable…something we could brag about to our grandkids.

It was turning out to be quite a restful and enjoyable week at the Harlequin and our days were pretty much free. Some of us ate with the theater company in residence; it was fun to hang out with actual, professional actors and fascinating to hear first-hand stories of their life in the theater.

At one point in our travels, Traf came down to Florida to join me for a couple of days. After dinner and a glass or two of wine, she raised her glass to me in a toast saying, "Here's to our firstborn."

Our first child together…I was blown away!

Since our days were free, a few of us actually went to see the blockbuster movie *Close Encounters of the Third Kind* that was playing in movie houses across the country.

When I returned, I received a phone call from Kirch: "Traf called. She seemed pretty upset and needs you to call her." So, after getting Kirch's message I called home immediately.

Normally, Traf is pretty positive, but this time she was quite upset; even weepy. She had, unfortunately, miscarried. I'd heard that it's not uncommon with first pregnancies but that doesn't soften the blow when it happens to you!

I did my best to console, comfort, support, etc., but man… I'm on the phone a thousand miles away! I offered to fly home, but no; in her typical selfless way she immediately squashed the idea. *"No way!"*

She was committed to Matrix as much as the rest of us. That's who I married.

# 33

We were scheduled to play a one-nighter in Birmingham, Alabama on Monday, February 21, 1977. From there it was a reasonable hop to New Orleans where we stayed with Dietch's brother, Rick.

As luck would have it, the next day was Fat Tuesday– *Mardi Gras!* We had to check it out, of course. I can't remember who I was with (possibly Brad) but all I can say is, *"Ho—ly Shit!"*

You know, living in New York City for close to a decade, I saw plenty—I mean *plenty*—especially when it came to gay, cross-dressing, drag. But this was…different.

I mean, what I may have seen in New York was like a children's tea party compared to this outrageous parade of extremes. As a Midwesterner with a small-town upbringing, I wasn't ready for this. Definitely a case of "to each his own."

Okay. So I've experienced the event once, and that'll be enough for me. But before moving on I *should* say something about the crowds. The human press around me was *scary*. I'm talking about 'arms-pinned-to-the-side' scary! It literally took me forty-five minutes to go a quarter of a block away to a *bar…just to get a beer!*

Yikes! Not for the faint of heart… or the claustrophobic.

# 34

So, what *were* we doing with this unusual instrumentation that was according to a Leonard Feather review:

*"...adventurous, exciting, and just about totally new?"*

Well, first of all, almost all of our pieces were programmatic: they told stories or painted musical landscapes or portraits. Many of our original compositions were inspired by literary works: Fred's "Childhood's End," from Arthur C. Clarke's classic of the same name, and my pieces: "Balthazar," "Justine," "Mountolive," and "Clea" from Lawrence Durrell's *The Alexandria Quartet*.

Nature itself also inspired pieces, such as Zap's "Blue Snow," a delicate, exquisite little sound piece, or Tex's "Tale of the Whale," whose intro and ending, thanks to creative synthesizing and unique pedaling on the fretless bass, puts the listener 'under the sea.'

Then there was our use of voices as background color as opposed to the usual 'lead vocal' concepts. That definitely set us apart!

Moreover...and this is the big one, we had *phenomenal* musicians. To be able to pull off highly technical passages of dazzling power as well as gentle, subtle, whispered moments, this was no ordinary bunch; these guys were high-end brilliant and educated musicians!

And for me, one of the more thrilling aspects of being a member of this orchestra was *knowing* that after a performance, even if we were playing to a completely new audience, we would have a host of new Matrix fans. Guaranteed!

The lines waiting after concerts to get autographs and albums confirmed this night after night. I don't have any figures, but I do know we generated quite a bit of money through our concerts. The problem was we owed so much that we, as players, never saw but a fraction of what our performances earned.

But you know what? None of us seemed to mind. What does that tell you about their integrity and dedication to an ideal? In a society where success is predicated on a bank balance, these guys were pretty damned unique!

Think about it. Some were married with obligations, (I had a wife and a young son at home) and here we were running around the country, chasing an ideal! How can you not admire people like that? Then again, the pragmatists of the world might justifiably say, "What a bunch of bloody fools!"

Getting back to the musicianship aspect of our guys, often one of them would jokingly complain about some of the gnarly figures I might conceive; in other words, highly technical, difficult passages. The plaintiff might whine, "This might be easy on piano, but it's damned near impossible on the trumpet, trombone or saxophone or bass"…etc.

But guess what? To a man, they would work it out and then flawlessly execute the passage in question. Believe me, as the composer it was *heavenly* to be able to write for such dedicated players with which we were blessed!

It wasn't just the critics who'd praised us. For example, there was a night in Chicago where we were playing Joe Segal's Jazz Showcase. Our gig went late. As luck would have it, the Stan Kenton Band had an earlier concert somewhere nearby so at least a dozen members of the Kenton band showed up for our last set.

The joint was pretty packed, and we were primed. I don't want to exaggerate, but we pretty much kicked ass, resulting in a roaring standing ovation! The compliments from these guys were, of course, flattering; but more importantly, it confirmed and reaffirmed the validity of what we were doing.

When your peers are impressed—and this was no fly-by-night outfit, it was the Kenton Band after all!—well… it meant the world.

# 35

While Rod Stewart, Stevie Wonder, Barbra Streisand, and The Bee Gees were dominating the pop charts, *Star Wars*, *Rocky*, *Saturday Night Fever* were grabbing moviegoers. What about Matrix? We just kept grinding it out, doing our thing.

After Mardi Gras we motored to Kingsville, Texas, for a concert at Texas A&M. The following night was free, so we parked our vehicles, Starship and Moon Unit, and spent a fair part of the day and all night at Padre Island… on the beach!

During the evening, with the beer freely flowing, a spontaneous percussion jam occurred featuring Murph, of course, and Tex (a hell of a good drummer/percussionist), Chimp, a wonderful time-keeper on damned near anything, and Zap, the most versatile player in the band.

My percussion chops sucked but not my beer consuming (*chuckle*)! As a result, my memory gets a bit fuzzy here, but the event stayed with me, and years later we recorded "Padre Island Sunrise" on our *Proud Flesh* album.

Two days later we played La Bastille, a very hip jazz club in Houston. The very cool manager/owner and sweet guy, Randy Martin, really liked us. I mention this only because later on we would have an important week there.

From Houston, it was off to another biggie, the Reno Jazz Festival. I specifically remember this because I was slated to give a clinic at one of their many sites. I think it was just me doing the clinic, but I'm not positive.

What I *am* positive about is that Bobby Shew was presenting before me. He's not only a killer trumpet player, but also extremely knowledgeable, and articulate, and handsome, and…intimidating as all hell!

How do I follow that? Plus, the place is packed and they're hanging on his every word. He's cradling his flugelhorn and occasionally offering brilliant little improvised riffs that would qualify for the Smithsonian….

*Aarghhh*…I felt like the *incredible shrinking man!*

Well, when he finished, and after hordes of students shook his hand in adoration, I timidly introduced myself. As I recall, he was very welcoming and, having heard of Matrix (the word was out), was anxious to hear us first-hand.

I felt a bit less overwhelmed after chatting with him. Very cool guy and ridiculously good at what he did! "Get used to hanging with heavies like this," I thought.

Under Willard's wing, and with a growing confidence in what we were doing, again I thought, "Alright! Bring it on. I can do this clinic thing…"

I think my biggest fear was in representing Matrix appropriately. In truth I don't remember exactly what I talked about except, perhaps, I mentioned the vision I had for the band. Furthermore, in an impossible industry, I stressed that a bunch of no-name Midwesterners had begun to achieve things by dint of sheer hard work and *total* commitment.

I realize this may sound cliché; but we were *literally* doing just that! Of course, a bit of good luck didn't hurt along the way. Oh…and by the way, as scared as I was, whatever I presented that day, I'm still alive to talk about it.

After our performance at the festival, Bobby was very complimentary of our music. As it turns out, this would lead me to many wonderful music collaborations with him, as well as a lasting friendship.

Following the Reno experience, we headed back to California for a lovely series of gigs: Monterey Peninsula College, Eagle Rock High School, and a festival that featured Louis Bellson at Orange Coast College in Costa Mesa.

At the University of California-Berkeley several of us met up with former Lawrence University pal, Ginger Bevis. She was most hospitable, especially considering the water-rationing that was going on in California due to a prolonged drought.

When using the toilet, she instructed us with the following local directive: "When it's yellow, let it mellow. When it's brown, flush it down."

But the most memorable thing about staying with her was not so much about catching up with an old friend but laying around on her living room floor listening to music.

The band had recently purchased *Heavy Weather*, the new release from Weather Report, and we hadn't had the chance to listen to it yet. This was the album that featured "Birdland," which went on to become a national hit. I also remember being totally mesmerized by "The Juggler."

Good friend that she was, Ginger gracefully indulged us for basically taking over her living room. She seemed to understand how important this was to us. Thank you, Ginger.

This memorable tour finally culminated with an appearance in Los Angeles at the Easter Seal Telethon hosted by Michael Landon, star of *Little House on the Prairie*.

Whew! Time to head home.

# 36

It was late March. Disco was still bumpin' and grinding along and the baseball season was right around the corner.... Ahhh, spring!

Back home in Wisconsin we had a bunch of semi-local gigs, namely Milwaukee, Racine, and Appleton. It was a good time to regroup, get into some new material, and totally enjoy being home for a bit.

Being on the road has its fair share of unpleasantness: vehicle breakdowns, long trips, flat tires, snowstorms, etc. But there are also more than a fair share of humorous happenings. Here, then, is yet another of the goofy things that went down; this one involving our beloved Chimp.

\* \* \* \* \*

*We were somewhere in the southwest (California or Arizona) and it was steaming hot in the motorhome. We had a food/gas stop and then were on our way again.*

*As I said, it was unbearably hot. And I remember being overwhelmed by the powerfully pungent odor of...you guessed it... feces! Bad enough on its own, but in the heat, excruciating.*

*Well, our dear Chimp was wearing a brand new, short-sleeved, very yellow shirt. We were all moaning about the smell when Chimp got up to move to the back of the motorhome and, ah...! the tell-tale brown stain on his new shirttail solved the mystery.*

*On the pit stop, Chimp had relieved himself and then, without realizing, wiped his ass with his shirt tail! Only Chimp.*

\* \* \* \* \*

Jeff was dubbed 'Chimp' by Fred who was masterful at apply-ing nicknames to all of us. Chimp was a brilliant musician, but alas, was not blessed with naturally handsome physical features. He was short, kind of squat, continually fighting a weight problem.

And when screwing up his facial features a certain way, he looked remarkably close to a damned chimpanzee! Funny enough by itself, but he would often speak in huffing grunts, enhancing the 'Chimp' reference.

He was one of the kindest, gentlest souls combined with outstanding musical gifts…but was just one of those guys that happened to invite hilarity…often at his own expense.

# 37

After the Easter Seal Telethon we were able to be back home for a spell. 1977 would turn out to be a hell of a year for us. For one, Willard's negotiation with an RCA record deal was finally materializing. Secondly, the boys back in the Chicago office, especially Dennis, were putting together a nice tour.

Shortly after a performance at Lawrence University, we headed out for a new tour. The first engagement was on May 9 in Ada, Oklahoma, at East Central University. The following day Willard and I had a long conversation concerning the RCA deal. Things were heating up on that front as Willard *himself* was sitting down with the company's top echelon. Stay tuned!

Next stop, a beautiful four nights at Randy Martin's La Bastille in Houston, Texas. Randy was one of my favorite people and La Bastille was certainly one of my favorite gigs.

A quick aside: we hadn't been checked into the hotel *five minutes* when, returning to the motorhome, discovered that the television had been stolen! *Ahhh*, life in the big city.

The gigs at La Bastille were well-attended and enthusiastically received. We were, however, all starting to become a little anxious as there was still no word from Willard. Then it was on to Miami.

We were scheduled for another week at Joe Rico's Airliner Motel when we *finally* got the call from Willard. Great news! The deal was firm with RCA! He was calling from New York to request my presence; I asked that Herb and Zap be present as well.

So, the day after the Airliner gig, Herb, Zap, and I flew to New York City. RCA wanted to remaster our original *Ultra Nova* album that had been recorded at Vern Castle's Studio in Lake Geneva, Wisconsin and produced by Warren Kime.

Our hope was to take some percussion sections recorded *live* by Herb at one of our performances and electronically 'mix' them into the original recording. RCA agreed to give it a try.

The engineer who was nice, helpful, and efficient was able to seamlessly insert the live performance into Fred's "The Last Generation." It was beautiful! After the mix was completed there was a bunch of paperwork for me to sign and that was that.

We were now officially a recording artist on a major label! It was a great moment but also a relief to finally be able to shed the label 'best-band-to-not-have-a-record-deal.'

It was during this auspicious trip that I was able to visit my old friend and avant-garde artist, Steve Conley. I had lived with him for a couple of years when I moved to New York in 1960. Our friendship dated back to our college days, both of us having attended Lawrence College, now called Lawrence University.

An article in *Esquire* heralded Steve as one of New York's cutting-edge contemporary artists. I asked him if we could use one of his paintings for our cover art on the soon-to-be released album. He readily agreed and did all the necessary legwork to make it happen. For me at least, Steve's friendship and involvement with this project made *Matrix IX*, our debut RCA album, *extra* special.

That was one hell of a trip considering that mixing, signing, and cover art was all completed in roughly three days!

# 38

Some truly memorable gigs followed. At St. John's University, we opened for Dizzy—as in Gillespie! *Plus*, he *actually sat in* with us on his famous tune, "Manteca." The following night we split a concert with the group Soprano Summit led by saxophonist Bob Wilbur.

Bob liked us but his sidekick, clarinetist Kenny Davern (an old-school cranky bastard), complained to the traditional audience, "We don't need all these goddamn wires!"

He was obviously referring to our fairly elaborate sound system and definitely had the mentality of 'we don't flat our fifths; we drink 'em.' In other words, he was what was known as an old-school, moldy fig.

Following those dates, we spent several laughable days at an old, kind of dilapidated three-story house outside the rural town of Langhorne, Pennsylvania. Some of us lodged there for free and it seemed like the ideal situation, right?

The country setting sounds inviting, but alas, the area was fraught with ticks! Because of this, several members opted for the creature comforts of a nearby motel.

Those of us who stayed in the house didn't realize that, on the second floor, the home/club owner had a large pen with eight or nine puppies, Irish Setters, I believe.

Our host (whose name I don't recall) had this club in town called Truffles. This was the deal: stay for free, play a gig at his place *and*, if he liked us, we could work two or three more nights at his club.

As I remember, it was a kind of a biker bar and…as you might imagine, they didn't like us. We were all grateful that we didn't get the extended gig. The only positive thing I recall about our stay in Langhorne was the opportunity to rehearse in the downstairs "living room" …if you could call it that!

The smell of puppies and dog shit have stayed with me all these years. Stay tuned. We went from ridiculous to sublime.

# 39

As bad as Langhorne was, our next appearance was golden. In Silver Spring, Maryland we were scheduled to do a whole week at the Showboat Lounge opening for legendary guitarist, Joe Pass! As beautiful as this may sound, the situation did *not* start well.

We had already set up but, when Joe came into the stage area, he took one look and snarled, "What the fuck is this? I book only solo, period!" Well, in a huff, he bolted to call his manager wanting to cancel the date. Whatever his manager said, Joe came back reluctantly, and in a pretty pissy mood.

Then Herb set up Joe's monitor for a sound check with one of our Bose speakers. His mood warmed considerably; he *totally* loved the sound that Herb provided for him.

So Matrix opened the show and, after he actually heard us and what we were doing, his attitude did a complete 180°. We opened on Monday and by Wednesday we were *"the best goddamned band on the scene!"*

What started out as a pretty sour situation turned out to be a killer week. We were told that Joe, so impressed with our Bose system, went right out and bought one for himself.

After the Showboat Lounge we returned home to Wisconsin for a few days. It was time to gear up for a real major: the Newport in New York Jazz Festival! Think about it: Monterey and Newport in the same year!

Because of the magnitude of the occasion, Traf and I decided to drive separately from the band so we could bring along our six-year-old son, Jason. This was too big of a deal to not have them share in the experience.

Unfortunately, we had a bit of a beater for a car. As bad luck would have it, our alternator went out late at night somewhere in Pennsylvania. Stopping at a gas station (thank God one was open!), the guy manning the pumps knew of a friend who he thought could fix it. He knew the address of the mechanic in question and told us how to get there.

Obviously, we couldn't shut the engine off now and risk not getting it started again. We were able to find the mechanic's place and by that time it was 2:00 a.m. or so. We took a bold chance by parking in his driveway and then tried to get some sleep.

By early morning, a rap on the window awakened me with a shock. I mean, the guy comes out to get the morning paper and here's a car with Wisconsin plates in his driveway! I braced for the worst and got out of the car stammering an explanation for our seemingly brazen behavior.

The man had a kindly look, saw Traf and Jason, and assured me he would do the best he could to help us out. You can imagine my relief! He not only didn't call the police but actually offered to help! What an angel this man turned out to be!

I still, to this day, swell with gratitude when I chance to think of that wonderfully kind man. And oh, by the way, he fixed the alternator and charged us such a minimal amount (somewhere around $35) that I figured he must have felt sorry for us.

So we paid him (I think with a check) and after many heartfelt "thank yous," we were on our way again.

Note to self: Get a better car!

Second note to self: There *are* good people out there in the world.

# 40

Leading up to Newport, we had a couple of dates, one at Edinboro State College in Edinboro, Pennsylvania, *and* at Cooper River Stadium, Pennsauken, New Jersey. Our date at Newport in New York was scheduled on July 1, and it was pretty steamy in the city.

Wouldn't you know, our beater of a car started overheating! We certainly didn't need another car issue with such an important gig looming. To ease the situation temporarily, we ended up putting some 'gunk' in the radiator. There were much bigger fish to fry!

Tired and sweaty, we finally arrived at Avery Fischer Hall, home of the New York Philharmonic and prepared for our sound check. We were on stage when I was shocked to hear a demanding directive from one of the unionized stage crew: *"Don't touch that!"*

What the hell? I was just going to adjust my piano seat, for God's sake!

Welcome to New York. Having lived in the city for a number of years I shouldn't have been surprised.

Herb, of course, was pissed at the hall's *very unionized* sound man who wouldn't let him do a damn thing! This meant that all the nuances of our music, which Herb knew so well, would probably be neglected. With the exception of the program we presented, we had little or no say.

As it turned out we opened for Gato Barbieri, a popular tenor saxophone player of some reputation. We played what I thought was a killer set with our usual variety of material. I specifically remember the thrill of playing "Mount Olive", a highly energized piece that showcased the power of our brass section; with searing brass parts—Tex, Chimp, and Zap led the way.

The audience seemed receptive to our stuff as I recall. We took our bows and exited the stage. Willard was backstage and called me over to introduce me to the well-known jazz entrepreneur, George Wein. Mr. Wein was quite complimentary, and this seemed to please Willard.

The next day however, Willard was summarily pissed; we got the only 'less than rave' review we ever received. The reviewer questioned why a "trendy rock band from Wisconsin" was hired when there existed dozens of more deserving New York musicians.

It was as though the reviewer had made up his mind before we even played a note. This was definitely an obvious case of New York chauvinism. No matter. We pretty much laughed it off because, by now…we knew *what* and *who* we were.

My only peeve was the "trendy rock band" reference; if any band was untrendy, (*chuckle*) it was us! And rock…? To this critic I say: "Young man, you may have a future in Waste Management!"

# 41

Somehow, despite the overheating issues with the car, we limped back to Wisconsin in one piece. On July 9, we were scheduled to appear at Milwaukee's annual Summerfest. But this time was different; we were finally given some regional recognition.

We were on the main stage opening for the headliner Les McCann. There was a huge crowd and they *loved* us! That day we opened a bunch of local eyes...*and* ears!

Schedule-wise though, it was a little awkward as we had to turn around and head back east to Cleveland. Our contract there called for clinics during the days and performances in the evenings. So, after packing up from Summerfest well after dark, we were to meet up by 10 p.m. or so and head east. Just another 'hit and run' all-nighter.

No biggie. On this particular sojourn, something pretty funny happened:

\* \* \* \* \*

*Tex, our lead trumpet (iron man), got his nickname from having been born in Texas, though he grew up primarily in Oklahoma. Except for his trumpet virtuosity, Tex was wired 'slow'; he never seemed to rush into anything.*

*If he couldn't remember an incident that we were reminiscing about, his favorite slow-mo response was, "I must have been smashed." In life's journey, Tex's "allegro" was more like "adagio non troppo."*

*So anyway, we assembled fairly late that evening and headed toward Chicago. Tex, who had no driving responsibility that night, laid down in the back of the motorhome.*

*He looked out the window and saw a sign which read: Chicago, 30 miles. With that he turned off the world and went to sleep.*

*We drove through the night arriving outside Cleveland fairly early in the morning. It was my job to call the contact person and make arrangements for setting up.*

*For some reason, we'd never gotten word from the office that the Cleveland dates had been canceled! Nothing to do but turn around and head back to Wisconsin. Stuff happens.*

*Meanwhile, Tex was still sleeping peacefully. By the time he surfaced, he peered out the window and saw a sign that read: Chicago, 30 miles. Hmmm…"I must have been smashed."*

\* \* \* \* \*

After the infamous, somewhat hilarious (thanks to Tex) Cleveland snafu, we had a date in Kansas City, Missouri at Brush Creek Park. The only notable thing about the gig was that we performed on what was called a 'showmobile,' a portable stage on the back of a semi-trailer.

Not exactly hall-of-fame quality after Avery Fischer Hall, New York City. A gig's a gig, I guess.

# 42

For a short spell we didn't have any dates booked by Willard. This was a good time to rid ourselves of the road grime and work in Brad as our newest member. These local gigs were a good opportunity to acclimate him to our way of doing things.

Being from Rockton, Illinois where his parents ran a farm, I'm sure he welcomed the chance to visit home as well as get comfortable with his new Matrix family.

'Barry,' as he became known, was a perfect fit for us. Not only was he a superb bass trombone player but a high-quality, cool guy as well. Being brought up on the farm, Brad had the Midwestern work ethic plus a real understanding of mechanical things.

Back in Appleton, we had the luxury of being able to rehearse during the day at Josef's. Thanks to the owner, Russell Josef, we also got to perform a couple of nights there as well. He *loved* us; when we played there the place was always packed. What was not to love?

This was a perfect time for Brad to get comfortable with the book and for me to dig into some new material.

\* \* \* \* \*

*When Fred left Matrix, we were sorry to see him go but, at the same time, we were happy for him. We knew he was soon to be married to the love of his life.*

*On August 6, all members of the band gathered with other guests and family to witness this special event. Blue skies, sunshine, light breeze…it was an absolutely perfect day for an outdoor wedding.*

*Folding chairs were set up on either side of the grassy aisle and Fred stood at the head of it, waiting for his beautiful bride to appear. He'd hired a brass quintet to play pre-wedding music, plus he had written a special processional for the occasion.*

*When Fred's 'special piece' began, it meant that Suzy was to begin walking in. She looked radiant!*

*Fred had prearranged something 'out of the ordinary' with the quintet: when Suzy was halfway up the aisle, the musicians broke into the first strain of "If You Knew Suzy, Like I Know Suzy…"*

*Oh my! That's when she totally caved in…and burst out laughing! Only Fred could provide such a humorous twist to a normally solemn occasion!*

*Shortly after tying the knot with his lovely lady, he would launch his incredible education/composing career.*

\* \* \* \* \*

On the August 22, we left for Colorado. Not only were we scheduled to perform at the Telluride Jazz Festival August 26-28, but we were also hired to provide sound for the entire festival.

The event was held in a box canyon in the Rockies some 11,000 feet above sea level. We were warned to be somewhat cautious with alcohol consumption since very thin air could lead to a quicker buzz than usual.

Because of the heavy responsibility of having to provide sound for a festival of this size, Herb brought in longtime friend Chris Lund as a second roadie. The extra help would be invaluable with the complexity of a 32-channel Bose system.

Chris was one of the nicest guys on the planet; soft-spoken, hardworking, and always on the ready should anyone need something on the stage. Now we had a crew of three: Herb, sound genius, loveable Lauben, also hardworking and a great Packer fan (like me), and now Chris who soon earned a new 'name.'

Let's say we're in the deep South; it's hotter than hell outside; there's not a lot of air circulating in the motorhome; pungent odors become magnified. For obvious reasons, Chris, this gentle guy, became known as 'Stink Foot.'

Our discomfort was a small price to pay considering the value he brought to the table. No way could we have done any better. This brings up a somewhat unusual arrangement when it came to housing on the road. It's still something that brings on a warm chuckle when I think about it.

With twelve of us, lodging could be damned expensive and we had debts to consider: Sonart (lawsuit), lease for the Starship, equipment truck payments, booking commissions…you get the idea.

So this is how it worked: kind of a birds-of-a-feather approach. We would pull into a motel and order three rooms; yes, I said *three*, never making it quite clear to the clerk the actual number of 'guests' to be housed. We designated four to a room with very special assignments.

The rooms were appropriately named: "The Stones" for those whose habits include regular indulgence in herbal substances (is that how 'Herb' got his moniker?); "The Mids" for those who were more casual, occasional 'participants', and "The Straights" for obvious non-participants.

This is in no way judgmental, but an impromptu visit to "The Stones" room could result in a secondhand buzz from the blue haze that permeated the place. I 'Plead the Fifth' as far as *who* resided *where*. I'm guessing you, the reader, will figure it out as we get on with it.

Ah…boys will ever be boys.

# 43

Telluride was a stunning experience in just about every way: wonderful music with a variety of iconic jazz figures including stars like Gary Burton, Hank Jones, Chick Corea, Dizzy Gillespie, Cecil Taylor, etc.

It was somewhat difficult to get oneself 11,000 feet above sea level to this picturesque place, but the setting alone was *so* worth the effort! In addition to the variety of jazz artists, the mountain setting with its shimmering aspens was memorable.

*Ahhh*...Telluride, this semi-restored old mining town, had more than its share of Old Western charm, a wonderful setting for such an event. Everything about the festival was fascinating to me.

Crowds were large and enthusiastic. And of course, the music was thrilling! It really doesn't get much better than that. In all, we appeared three separate times at Telluride.

In 1977 and 1979, I witnessed two titans of total contrast, polar opposites in the extreme! One of the perks of doing a festival like Telluride was meeting and hanging with artists you admire. There was an artists' tent near the stage with the usual snack items plus beer, wine and, oh yeah, soda and water...

It was there that I had a totally unlikely, but delightful, meeting with one of my personal favorites—legendary blues guy, Muddy Waters.

My oh my! What a supremely cool character! Forty-five minutes before Muddy went on, he sat quietly while an attendant (presumably a road manager) served him an endless supply of champagne in the appropriate stemware.

After meeting him I continued to watch as he calmly greeted people. They paid homage in a variety of fashions from a simple handshake to fawning adoration. He answered their questions politely (an attitude that made me admire him even more) but he seemed to prefer withdrawing into his own private world.

What a totally cool guy! Like nothing short of an earthquake or tsunami would raise his pulse. He must have been in his eighties, and I wondered if he had the energy to perform.

His trio went out onstage to warm up the crowd with a couple of toe-tappers. And then the emcee introduced him and, with seemingly amused indifference, Muddy slowly made his way to the microphone.

Then the magic happened! This gentle, soft-spoken blues artist went out and kicked *serious ass* to the frenzied delight of the crowd! I was blown away with his energy as he rocked through blues after blues—as naturally as falling off a log.

The huge crowd went nuts! I thought to myself 'If this isn't fun, I don't know what is!' Muddy Waters! 'Gimme some o' that!'

By contrast, at another appearance at Telluride in 1979, I met the other-worldly, avant-garde pianist, icon of so-called 'free-jazz,' Cecil Taylor. Compared to Muddy Waters, I remember Cecil Taylor as being much more socially accessible off-stage, both friendly and engaging. He was soft-spoken, affable…easy-going.

I remember talking with him about the New York Mets, the price of gas (65¢ a gallon?!), etc. We discussed everyday stuff, as casually as any good next-door neighbor.

*Then he went on stage!* He was like some kind of alien from another galaxy…a keyboard maniac with two-fisted chord clusters, crashing dissonance, virtuosic cascades of atonal runs, all totally improvised…definitely *not* your garden-variety smooth jazz guy!

His style of playing, though shockingly impressive, often left me reaching for the aspirin bottle. He may not be my everyday cup of tea but I still find him fascinating; a kind of musical Jekyll and Hyde.

\* \* \* \* \*

*During our travels, on one occasion we narrowly avoided disaster. Picture us blithely whizzing along on some county road and suddenly, without warning, we hear a siren from a police car and see his red lights flashing menacingly!*

*Uh-oh! What the hell are we being stopped for?*

*Whomever was driving pulled off the road and stopped, while the rest of our collective pulse spiked up. The officer came into our motorhome and asked, "What's the height of this vehicle?"*

*Someone responded with "Twelve-foot-six, sir" (Not sure of the accuracy of that). "Well," the officer responded, "maybe a quarter of a mile up the road, there's a railroad trestle that's only eleven feet high! You better find a different route!"*

*We gratefully thanked him for averting what could have been a very real disaster! Whew!*

\* \* \* \* \*

From Telluride it was on to Wyoming for a concert at Western Wyoming College in Rock Springs. After the performance we looked for a place to hang in town. We stopped at a bar and stepped inside to check it out.

I guess we should have known better when we pulled into the parking lot and saw nothing but pickup trucks: the bar was noisy, jammed with cowboys packing and, oh yeah…hookers.

We did a quick about-face and beat a hasty retreat to the relative safety of our vehicles.

Time to move on.

# 44

And move on, we did! Gigs in Salt Lake City, and Ridgecrest and Bakersfield, California, led to our *second* appearance at the Monterey Jazz Festival in as many years. Not many bands could make that claim!

Jimmy Lyons was cool. And as you may recall, he was the host of the National Collegiate Jazz Festival; he had *raved* about the original music we'd played with the Lawrence University Jazz Ensemble way back then.

Next, we were headed to the Great American Music Hall in San Francisco. We headed the Starship south on Pacific Coast Highway 1 along the coast. As we blissfully headed out, we "oohed and aahed" at the dramatic views of the Pacific Ocean. However, it soon turned dark and we really had no clue what we were in store for.

\* \* \* \* \*

*Perhaps five or six miles north of San Francisco the road began a pretty steep descent. There were harrowing switchback turns dangerously close to the drop-off coastline some 150 feet below.*

*The moon shone brightly so the drop-off was in clear view. The surf pounded against the rocky shoreline, and I admit it was a spectacular view. But scary as hell!*

*To make matters worse, Chimp, who as noted earlier, had a very low tolerance for pain (or the prospect of it) freaked us all out with his audible, fear-laden grimacing!*

*At all of the left-turn switchbacks the back of the motorhome was literally left hanging out over the edge, accompanied by one of Chimp's fearful moans.*

*As the driver, Zap somehow kept his cool despite Chimp's whimpering, and he did a masterful job negotiating this treacherous descent. But then we got a frightening, kind of panicky call from the Moon Unit that was trailing us. "Zap! You gotta pull over at the nearest opportunity! Your brakes are smoking!" Yikes. And yes...at that point we could smell it.*

*Obviously, on such a terrifying descent, the last thing you want is for your brakes to fail. The only course of action was to pull over and let them cool down before venturing on which, of course, we did.*

*And we luckily lived to tell about it.*

\* \* \* \* \*

You know, I didn't have any gray hair at the time, but I wouldn't be surprised if I sprouted a few during that little episode.

Our appearance at the Great American Music Hall in San Francisco was especially important for two reasons: first of all, this was a renowned venue which we were excited about playing.

Second, our show (as today's gigs are referred to) led to a conversation with a very enthusiastic member of the audience. Up to this point, we still hadn't found a suitable replacement for our bassist, Randal Fird.

We happened to mention that we needed a bass player and he asked us where our next job was. When we said Santa Barbara, his eyes lit up, and he excitedly told us about this "monster player" from there.

Turns out, the guy we were talking to was *from* Santa Barbara, knew the scene well, and urged us to look up Randy Tico.

Often good fortune occurs as the result of bad news. As luck would have it, a high school concert in Paradise, California was canceled, leaving us with a couple of extra days before our gig at the Santa Barbara Bowl.

When we arrived in town we asked around about Randy and found out that he was playing at a joint called Baudelaire's. We were scheduled to do a noon concert in downtown Santa Barbara and, by chance, Randy happened to be there.

That night several of us went to Baudelaire's to check him out, and yes…he *was* a monster! I remember talking with him between sets and was struck by his enthusiasm, friendliness, and all-around (in California parlance) positive vibe.

When we identified ourselves and offered him an audition, he was quick to agree as he had *really* liked what he'd heard. Subsequently, we invited him to the Santa Barbara Bowl where we were to perform.

We set up our gear and invited him to jam with us. With no chart we started with a funk groove. Eight bars in we were all smiling and looking at each other. He was laying down some absolutely dangerous shit on his fretted bass! Murph was beside himself with joy!

There was no doubt this was our guy if he, in fact, agreed. Randal Fird was a wonderful, lyrical player whom we all loved; but he had had enough of the road and we all accepted the fact.

But Tico! Oh my! Ultimately, he would push us *all* to another level. And thankfully, he was 'all in' when we offered him the job. It was so exciting to speculate about the musical possibilities of the future with a killer player like Randy.

In many ways it would change the direction of the band. We were all pretty-well fired up thinking about what was to come.

# 45

Once Randy agreed to join us it was back to business. The Santa Barbara Bowl is a lovely outdoor venue which could accommodate several thousand patrons. I mentioned we had played a free noon concert in the downtown area to help promote the bowl gig.

We also, again to help advertise our upcoming performance, played another freebie at a local junior college. It was a good faith act on our part, not a booked engagement.

As far as our evening performance at the bowl, the local promoter dropped the ball. In other words, he hadn't done his job. This meant putting up posters, airing our recordings on local radio (our RCA records were available), giving live radio interviews (usually with me), etc.

As we'd seen in other new venues, that was the usual Willard formula that worked extremely well.

The night of our concert was a beautiful Santa Barbara evening. Everything seemed to suggest another Matrix triumph. Except for one thing: nobody came. I mean twenty to thirty people in a facility that could seat two to three thousand?

Well, it was pretty much a disaster (at least financially) for the promoter. Oh, we played our stuff just fine, but at the end of each piece it was almost like the sound of 'one hand clapping!'

Then came the 'fun' part. It was usually my job to contact the person in charge, answer any questions, relay our electronic needs, etc. and oh…yeah, after the performance collect the bread.

So I went backstage and was faced with our portly host, drunk on his ass, and scowling at me like I was the most vulgar piece of shit on the planet. He humiliated me with the snarls of an enraged dog.

I wasn't ready for *this*. He berated me and the band, but especially me, and threatened not to pay up. Well, I wasn't about to walk away empty-handed, especially after two free concerts to help spread the word!

Hell, we did *our* part and I *told him so!*

With an agonizingly long, baleful stare, he opened his checkbook and scrawled out the amount agreed upon. He didn't hand me the check but just kind of threw it at me. It silently fluttered to the cement floor. But all *I* wanted to do was get the hell out of there.

I had to semi-grovel to pick it up. Totally humiliated and emotionally defeated, I slinked away. Concerned that I had been in there so long, sweet Chris Lund had come to find me.

I saw the worry on his face and just lost it, bawling like a child who had just lost his dog. Chris put his arm around me and we walked back to the Starship where the guys anxiously awaited my return.

As bad as I felt, I will never forget the gentle, consoling support Chris offered me that bizarre night.

*The Equipment Truck*

**Back row:** *Bud Brisbois, Larry Darling, Brad McDougall, Jeff Pietrangelo, Mike Murphy, Randy Tico*
**Front row:** *Mike Hale, John Kirchberger, John Harmon, Doug Laughtenschlager, Kurt Dietrich*

*Matrix in front of Beggar's Tune (Appleton, Wisconsin), ca. 1979*

*John Harmon and son Jason (age 7) at Shade Tree Studio*
*Lake Geneva, Wisconsin, August 1978.*

*Jeff "Chimp" Pietrangelo's suggestions always seemed so on-the-money, and when screwing up his facial features a certain way, he looked remarkably close to a chimpanzee.*

*Matrix stayed at a truly unique motel along the Pacific Coast highway called Mina's in Redondo Beach, California, where Matrix played Concerts by the Sea in 1976-77.*

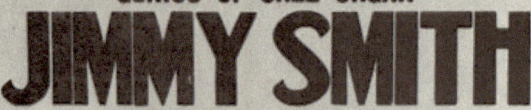

*Jazz Showcase (Chicago, Illinois), July 1978*

*Mike "Miff" Murphy in full "kick–ass" mode with his "magic shoe."*

*Herb Butler, sound engineer. Herb's "real" thing was sound. He was brilliant.*

*"Quack Factor" by Mike "Tex" Hale*

*Sometimes on long road trips, a person could go stir crazy.*
*"Tex" often kept himself occupied by drawing nonsensical characters!*

*Matrix Reunion, May 16, 2017, Appleton, Wisconsin*

**Back:** *Mike Hale*
**Middle:** *Randy Tico, John Harmon, Larry Darling, Brad McDougall*
**Front:** *Kurt Dietrich, John Kirchberger, Doug Lautenschlager*

# 46

Considering that the current tour began at the end of August, and the Santa Barbara debacle brought us to the end of September, and with most of October still booked in front of us, let's just say this was one hell of a long haul.

\* \* \* \* \*

*It was a late Sunday morning somewhere in southern California when we made a breakfast/gas stop. Dietch and I wandered into a drugstore looking for some postcards. We found the card carousel and were peering at it intently when, without warning, the carousel creaked and slowly turned—taking away our view of those cards that we were interested in.*

*We both peeked around the other side of the carousel only to discover a wizened old codger turning the device, completely oblivious to us, and our needs.*

*Rather than express irritation over the insensitivity of the old fart, Dietch uttered a nonsensical catchword of mine: "PHRAHNK!"*

*I don't know why, but the absurdity of the situation had me doubled over with compressed laughter, like a school kid trying not to draw attention to himself during class.*

*It still brings a smile after all these years.*

\* \* \* \* \*

Though the Santa Barbara Bowl fiasco was unfortunate, we had scored a major plus when Randy Tico agreed to join us. He loved the musical direction we were headed in and was loaded with a positive vibe that was both infectious and welcome.

As we had a month left on this particular tour, Randy came along playing on pieces that he kind of 'learned on the fly' through the gracious help of Randal Fird. After Randy learned a piece he would sit in on the live performances when he felt comfortable. He was a quick study; a tribute to his phenomenal, intuitive musicianship.

Moreover, he also brought a fresh new energy to our stuff.

# 47

Following Santa Barbara, we played the Russian River Festival in northern California. A cancellation in Los Angeles gave us a few days outside of Guerneville, where we enjoyed some touch football, frisbee tossing, and wandering among the incredible, ancient redwoods. It was a wonderful, relaxing respite from the usual exhaustion of touring.

After that little break it was back to Redondo Beach for another three nights at Concerts by the Sea! I was especially happy because my sister, Anne, lived there; it was great to be able to connect and catch up.

From there we worked our way south with a bunch of cool college dates that included a memorable appearance on October 2 at the Laguna Music Festival. From there we had play dates in Mesa and Scottsdale, Arizona followed by another highlight: a concert at the community auditorium in the very artsy town of Taos, New Mexico. What a wonderful place, Taos!

Two days later we were in Seguin, Texas for a date. Another two days after that we pushed on to Fort Worth, opening for Buddy Rich at the Tarrant County Convention Center on October 13. We opened again for the Buddy Rich Band with two more gigs: one in Tulsa and one in Winfield, Kansas.

These were memorable for a couple of reasons: one, it was fun to hang with another touring band, comparing notes, exchanging phone numbers, etc., and two, discovering what an asshole Mr. Rich was! A great musician, but a real jerk. A dear friend who had toured with Buddy related how he fired the entire band on stage at a performance!

Our appearances with him will always stand out for one very special reason: Dennis Justice shared with me a particularly fascinating phone conversation with Buddy, who had initiated the call.

Referring to Matrix, he said something like this:

"Don't ever book me with these mother****ers again! You got that? They're stealing all of my thunder..." (expletive...expletive...expletive...)

Classy, eh?

After that, it was back to Wisconsin for some local dates and home cooking!

# 48

Our long stints on the road served to amplify how much I missed my wife and son. So, you can understand how I looked forward to the prospect of getting home for a while. Every week, I wrote at least one letter to Jason and made it a point to call home.

Recently, I was touched when Jason's wife, Melissa, shared with me that he had saved *every* letter I wrote. (He still has them to this day).

As much as I loved what we were doing, it was *wonderful* to get home! Traf was totally supportive of the band and my vision for it. As a superb musician herself with a keen, critical ear, she consistently gave us high marks. We probably wouldn't have made it as a couple without her unconditional support.

Consider this: she was raising an adopted boy from my failed marriage along with managing the endless slings and arrows of running a household alone. But she was *all in*.

I will always be grateful for her Olympic support. She definitely qualifies for sainthood on the first ballot!

To this day she still carries a deep affection for what we did.

# 49

With travel time after quite a lengthy tour, we perhaps had only five or six days at home. See what I mean about sainthood? We got home on October 20 and the next day we had a clinic/concert at the university in my hometown of Oshkosh, Wisconsin.

This was Randy's first full concert with us.

What an incredible force he brought to the game! He and Murph gave us such rhythmic excitement that they truly put us at a higher, more dynamic level than ever before. Add to that, Randy's exceptional creative soloing...*man*, as a band, we were hanging onto a tiger by the tail!

And please understand, this takes nothing away from the unique musical voice of Randal Fird. They were simply two different animals: Randal's contributions were sensitive. He was quiet, gentle, intellectual, and *totally* laid back; Randy, on the other hand, was energetic, dynamic, talkative (did I say *talkative?*) and utterly enthusiastic! You get the picture.

We all loved Randal and hated to see him go but it was easy to like Randy and admire his considerable gifts. We would grow to love him as well.

Moving along, we did some regional gigs and rekindled local relationships. But just like that, in what seemed the blink of an eye...we were back in Miami at the Airliner for two more nights starting on October 28.

After the Airliner we played a wonderful gig at the University of Miami in Coral Gables, then headed to New Orleans for four more memorable nights at the famous Rosie's.

Converted from a former mansion in the famous garden district of New Orleans, Rosie's was the trend-setting jazz venue in a city that was abundantly rich in jazz establishments. It was an amazing place to play, but what I remember *most* was a lounge that was separate from the performance area.

In the lounge one could sip a beverage in luxurious swings whose ropes were maybe thirty to thirty-five feet long, hung from the trusses of the building! Talk about unique!

Two nights after closing at Rosie's, we drove to New Harmony, Indiana, then on to Houghton, Michigan, and finally to Baldwin, Kansas! What the hell were those agents doing? Throwing darts at the map? *Sheesh!*

Maybe you've heard of guys in bands getting disoriented on the road; this is a perfect example of why that can happen. It's also the reason that some bands break up during rigorous touring. That kind of scheduling can stretch tolerances to the limit...*and* beyond. Though occasional minor differences would flare up, to our credit, *nothing could dissolve the bonds created by this brotherhood and its singleness of purpose.*

I know it showed in the way we played...pretty much blowing audiences away wherever we appeared.

# 50

Earlier, I mentioned the importance of a record deal for obvious reasons: it helped an artist weave through the maze of industry-locked doors, opening them, gaining publicity, earning credibility, etc.

And through Willard's weight as a world leader in the music biz, we were able to realize that goal. We signed with RCA Victor for $35,000, a seemingly astronomical sum.

Of course, we never actually *saw* much of that money owing to our debt to Willard. Remember that he had bailed us out of the Sonart mess. On top of that, there were motorhome lease payments, equipment truck payments... you get the picture.

Frankly, the bread (for us individually) was not the main issue here. We needed this record deal like a writer needs to publish. Moreover, this was RCA Victor, a *major* label! This was a ticket to more buyers, more promoters, more club owners hiring us. It also made the booking agent's job much easier. They didn't have to sell an 'unknown' to a prospective buyer.

Add to this situation, the very positive review of our new album in *DownBeat*, the veritable 'Bible of the jazz world.' We received a three-and-a-half-star rating (out of five) which was more than decent for a first release.

Mind you, critics always seem a tad reticent on reviews of first albums. We also know that most critics don't play professionally, but they *do* influence their readers. In any case, there were many positive things said about our record.

More importantly, the 'trades' such as *Billboard*, *Metronome*, *Variety*, and other industry magazines had given us *real* credibility. People could now read about us nationally. That was big!

And RCA, as expected, issued promotional ads in all the trades, announcing our debut album, *Matrix IX* (The IX was added at the advice of an attorney to protect us from any possible ownership by another band of the name Matrix). All systems go!

We all know the phrase, timing is everything. *Uh huh.* It just so happened that another "artist" (I use the term quite loosely, and I confess to a negative perspective on the person in question) was also on RCA's roster. That person was none other than...Elvis!

That's right. Elvis, as in Presley.

I implied that timing can have such a bearing on events; and nothing I can think of had more impact on us than what happened: *to the day*, one week after the release of our debut album, Mr. Presley cashed out, bought the farm, went to the other side!

His passing sent the entire RCA army into a frenzy of twenty-four-seven reproduction of Elvis product. 'Round the clock, I had heard.

*Arhhhhg!!!*

We never heard another word from the people at RCA. Whatever promotion they may have planned on our behalf... went into the dumpster.

"Shit" was about all we could think or say. As I said, 'timing'...the fortunes of, not war, but the music biz.

# 51

With much more zig-zagging between midwestern venues, we finished the tour at the Ivanhoe Theatre in Chicago on November 23, 1977. Noteworthy about the Ivanhoe gig was opening for the Thad Jones/Mel Lewis Band.

The band that evening was fronted by clarinetist, Buddy DeFranco because Thad was absent for the gig (I believe he was in Sweden where he eventually died). I personally loved Thad's writing, having programmed a number of his charts while heading up the jazz program at Lawrence. So, for me it was a memorable night, but somewhat odd with Mr. DeFranco at the helm.

Then we headed home for some much-needed R&R. After a couple of local gigs, we again headed south, this time back to Miami with no routing dates to break up the insane length of the trip.

You know, when you travel by motor vehicle it takes a while to get to Florida. And when you finally get to Pensacola in northern Florida, you think, 'What the hell. This wasn't so bad.' Seven hours later you're still not to Miami! It takes forever to get there!

It was early December. We were scheduled for a couple of weeks at another Joe Rico joint, The Checkmate Lounge. On a location gig like this, it turned out we had a night off during the week.

Looking for something fun to do, a few of us (including my wife who had joined us for a few days) took the motorhome down to the Keys. We ended up sleeping in the motorhome in a parking lot after spending the afternoon *and* evening at the Tiki Bar in Islamorada, Florida.

At the outdoor seating with soft ocean breezes, cold St. Pauli Girl beer, continuous jazz flowing from the PA system...*aaahh*...not a bad way to go. Sitting outside in shirtsleeves, it was quite a welcome change from the frigid north.

For nearly *two weeks* we were in the same place! What a luxury! The club was nice, crowds were cool and appreciative; all in all, it was a *very* pleasant time. I was always happy for our sound man and roadies: Herb, Lauben, and Chris during a location gig like this; once all the equipment was set up, their days were pretty much free until performance time.

Let me tell you something...these guys worked their asses off, especially on hit and run gigs: set up for a concert, play concert, tear down, travel the night, arrive in a new town, set up, play the concert, tear down, travel the night...

String half a dozen of those dates together and it's hard to keep track of what day it is.

But at concert time you walk on stage and, like magic, everything's beautifully in place! Lauben and Chris were always at the ready should we need *anything*.

I totally admire and love these guys. Herb, Lauben, Chris; what a blessing they were!

Speaking of Herb, I want to take a minute to pay tribute to a genius sound man. He was a fairly successful musician, having been co-leader of a group back in his home state of Minnesota.

*But his real thing was sound*...and the balance and blend of same. He was brilliant! Plus, his understanding of music (especially considering the complexity of our stuff) virtually made him a tenth member of the band.

He knew our book as well as we did and, as a result, was able to feather musical nuance into our presentation with such sensitivity. As a musician, what a blessing!

I mean, whatever the hall, gym, outdoor venue...he made us sound glorious. The guy was an unbelievable wizard! A lot of our success was due to Herb's uncanny skill. We played the music; he organized, blended, tweaked, and created a soundscape of elegant art.

Rest well, old friend.

# 52

When you put on as many miles as we did, bad luck is occasionally bound to happen. Matrix experienced a kind of 'Bermuda Triangle' phenomenon in or near North Platte, Nebraska. Interstate 80 goes pretty much through the flattest, scenically least interesting swath of terrain in the country.

But somehow serendipity fates had it in for us and fashioned three (count 'em...*three*) vehicle breakdowns within a fifty-mile radius! Twice the Moon Unit had issues, and later our bus had something go ka-flooey, again near North Platte.

On one of the unfortunate Moon Unit malfunctions, we happened to be homeward bound. We were all totally looking forward to reconnecting, enjoying some R&R, and the comfort of familiar environs.

Sadly, the truck was in need of serious repair and would require a couple of days' worth of attention. This meant an agonizing delay of the homecoming we had all so anticipated.

But ahhh...we had loveable Lauben who stepped up in true Mighty Mouse fashion with a *"Here I come to save the day!"* He definitely showed some 'take one for the team' character by volunteering to stay with the Moon Unit until repairs were completed.

This may not sound like such a big deal to you, the reader, but grinding it out for any length of time as we almost always did, the prospect of a little down time was to die for. Most of us were in the motorhome ready to leave.

I'll never forget waving goodbye to him as he stood outside his motel room. I felt so bad for him; it was close to heartbreaking.

Not to worry…Herb assured us with something like: "Ahhh, don't worry about Lauben. He's got enough money and especially enough weed to keep him happy for a week!"

Even so, Lauben goes down in my personal Hall of Fame for that incident…along with many more actions of pure generosity throughout our numerous adventures.

# 53

Like any other decade, there are issues of the profound as well as the casually absurd. In 1978, I recall being moved by the historic signing of the Camp David Accords brokered by President Jimmy Carter. That ended thirty-one years of war between Egypt and Israel. I also remember being shocked and horrified in November by the senseless mass-suicide in Jonestown, Guyana.

Here at home, I was so caught up in our goals for Matrix that domestic events and pop music held little or no interest for me. My leanings toward classical concepts, Native American culture, and new, expanded forms kept me pretty-well occupied. As a band we continued to find inspiration in the world music concepts of Weather Report.

After the holidays (1978), we began the New Year in Milwaukee on January 2 at Giorgi's. Then BAM! We were right back in the deep end of the pool, so to speak.

On January 7, we were featured at a concert in Dallas as part of the National Association of Jazz Educators. Kind of a big deal, I guess, but I have a personal bias when it comes to that organization.

Overall, the NAJE probably does good things when it comes to exposing students to the art form of jazz. But in my experience, many 'teachers of jazz' embraced, and taught, an often-limited view of the medium.

I mean, jazz is such an amazing musical language, that programming Buddy Rich charts or Maynard Ferguson, or even Count Basie, *doesn't* yield more than a glimpse of its incredible scope. Again, this is just my opinion.

\* \* \* \* \*

*On television and especially in movies, we've all been entertained by the tension created in staged, high-speed chases. That stuff never really happens in real life, right?*

*Think again…Covering the miles that we did, we were bound to see unusual events over time. In any case, I think we were in Texas, after a fairly long stretch of driving, when most of the guys wanted a lunch stop.*

*So, Dave Scott pulled into a large mall that had a McDonald's Restaurant, or 'Mac and Dons' as we referred to them (Yuck! I'm not much of a lunch person, so I took a pass and stayed on the bus with my nose in a book).*

*My reading was brutally interrupted by an extremely high-pitched whine of auto engines pushed to the max, accompanied by the screams of a siren. I spun around in my seat and saw a police car in hot pursuit of another vehicle.*

*I'm guessing they were both going at least 85 mph. The chase was on the very road that led into the mall! Whoa! What the hell?!*

*The fugitive veered into the massive parking lot where we were parked, maybe seventy or so yards in front of me. The driver must have hit the brakes hard as his car spun out of control and slammed a light standard, one of those fifty- or sixty-foot jobs.*

*I swear it was like slow motion as the damned thing slowly teetered ominously, and fell with a crash! It was close enough to me that I actually felt the aftershock.*

*'Is this really happening?' I wondered, my heart racing. The police car quickly pulled up followed by two or three gunshots! Oh boy! Next thing I knew, the fugitive got out, hands up.*

*Two armed police got the guy spread-eagled against his car, searched and cuffed him. Then they put him in the squad car and hauled him off.*

*Half in shock, I thought, 'Did this really just happen?' I couldn't tell if I was watching a TV show or actual life. I can still feel the thud of that light standard crashing down. The whole damned thing was totally 'surreal.'*

\* \* \* \* \*

After the NAJE and playing at Laredo Junior College in Texas, this particular tour took us to another memorable four nights at the well-known jazz room, La Bastille. Over time and a number of appearances there, Randy Martin, the club owner, became quite a friend and advocate. He was from New Orleans and I believe that it was on this trip that he invited us to his home and made authentic New Orleans gumbo.

*Whoowhee!*

The venue itself was nice, but what made the gig *so* special was sharing the date with two jazz luminaries: the Dave Liebman/Richie Beirach Duo! It was such a total gas hearing them and, of course, hanging with them as well.

I remember our last night there *particularly* because they both joined Matrix for a bit of a jam in the last set. We played one of our original pieces, "Balthazar," which we 'opened up' for solos by our guests.

Mr. Liebman was spinning his considerable musical magic when we cued in some fortissimo background shouts by our horn section. Our brass guys have the firepower to peel paint off a back wall when turned loose, and Dave wasn't ready for this.

With the first blast behind his solo, he literally *lurched* (and damn near fell over) as though someone had tossed a cherry bomb behind him! After his initial shock, he gathered himself, and finished off an energized, exciting solo.

A memorable moment which we all laughed about after the gig.

After La Bastille we played Nicholls State University in Thibodaux, Louisiana. That was then followed by dates in Tulsa, Oklahoma and Rolling Meadows, Illinois, and then home again. After our few days of recovering at home we headed back out…again. Seems like we were always leaving.

Two major developments happened sometime between the first of the year and mid-March of 1978: first, Dennis, our greatest advocate, left Willard's office as a booking agent. He and his friend/business partner, Phil Herring, took over the direction of Matrix with their new company named Seventh Mountain Management.

Phil, a very sweet guy, was formerly one of the bass trombone players with the Stan Kenton Orchestra. Willard and his army of agents would still do bookings, but Dennis and Phil would see to our career.

Second, Willard, with his uncanny negotiating skills, was cooking up another record deal for us…*this time* with Warner Brothers. Dennis shared with me the somewhat comical account of Willard's 'style.'

According to Dennis, who was present at the Warner Brothers meeting with Willard, Mr. Alexander pretty much took over the 'negotiation' in almost filibuster fashion. Every time Mo Ostin, president of Warner Brothers, opened his mouth, Willard interrupted with one unrelated anecdote after another.

After nearly two hours of this, Willard got up, shook hands with Mr. Ostin said, "It's always a pleasure doing business with a professional!" He then left the room, leaving

Mo wondering, 'What the hell did I just agree to?' Classic 'Willard,' according to Dennis.

For us, it ultimately meant a two-album deal: $80,000 for the first, and $90,000 for the second. Sheesh! Those kinds of numbers made my head spin.

For our part, before the deal was actually confirmed, we played a concert (I believe we opened for Woody Herman) but I don't recall where. What *was* important though was that a couple guys from Warner Brothers were sent to check us out. One was Mike Ostin (Mo's son), and the other, I'm pretty certain, was Ron Goldstein.

I was forewarned by Dennis and Phil that these guys were coming, and that I should talk with them after the gig. Then I was to call Dennis and apprise him and Phil of *exactly* what they said. A deal such as the one pending would mean a whole hell of a lot to all concerned!

After our performance I didn't have to seek them out; they came directly to me with an enthusiastic response to our program. They were dressed in what I would later recognize as 'California style': designer jeans, boots, Western style form-fitting shirts, and shoulder bags. Their positive review left me pretty optimistic that the deal would be firm.

And...hallelujah, it was! A huge boost and a bit of a reward for our hard work. Dennis and Phil were pretty fired up, as all of us were.

# 54

Subsequently, in March 1978 we headed to Lake Geneva, Wisconsin, for another recording session at Shade Tree Recording Studio, reuniting with our engineer-friend Andy Waterman (He was the same guy who was at the controls for our first session that became the RCA release, *Matrix IX*).

I didn't mention this before, but the Shade Tree Studio was physically a part of the Lake Geneva Playboy Club complex, bunnies and all! It was a strange dimension to the seriousness of the task that lay ahead.

We all stayed at the hotel which meant taking our meals in their restaurant. Breakfast was a bit surreal, what with these ludicrous bunny outfits, along with the equally ludicrous push-up bras that the girls had to wear.

Imagine ordering your eggs, "Two over easy please" with a pair of propped-up boobs staring you in the face! Is this what the fast lane looks like?

Hmm.

Apparently, Warner Brothers didn't quite trust our ability to manage a cohesive album's worth of material, so they sent John Simon, a well-known producer, to 'oversee' our project.

This was a little unsettling as we had always had total control of our music and we were more than a little anxious about a big-name industry guy telling us what to do. Incidentally, Mr. Simon was the musical director of the famous rock documentary *The Last Waltz*.

As it turned out John (Simon) was a very cool guy but we, as a group, got off to a bit of an uneasy start with him. March 21, the first day of recording, went well as we successfully recorded "King Weasel Stomp" and Fred's "Spring." This happened to be Fred's birthday *and*, since it was also the first day of spring, recording that particular piece seemed more than appropriate.

First day, two good takes; a good start. When I got back to my room there was a voice message: "Please meet with me in my room." It was John Simon's *invitation*…sounded ominous to me. We hadn't really gotten to know each other at this point so this 'meeting' left me feeling uneasy.

I went to his room and it's just the two of us. There I was…steeling myself for what??? John was nice, but firm, as he commented very favorably on the day's work. But then he expressed critical concerns about our 'centerpiece' composition, "Wizard."

That particular piece had taken us a couple of months to bring up to speed and all of us, roadies included, were excited to record it. The piece was lengthy, quite complex, a bit 'far out,' and, frankly, *hard as hell.*

Well…John Simon had serious reservations about recording "Wizard," which he referred to as "that *Clockwork Orange*" piece. I'm not usually the confrontational type, but I stood firm speaking up for the band. After all the hard work and collective creativity that went into it, I wasn't about to back down.

I explained to Mr. Simon how our band worked. Getting a new piece to the point of performance gave a revealing look at how we did things; it was the epitome of our collective creative method.

Sure, I wrote the notes, but elevating a piece to a performance-ready level was achieved by *everyone's* artistic input, not just mine. Sometimes this would lead to heated discussions about how to treat the various sections of a piece.

After hearing everyone's opinions we would finally agree on the best solution. We *all* had a voice in musical decisions until we arrived at a mutual consensus.

This concept was especially important in our rhythmic approach. Mind you, we had four guys with unbelievable percussion skills: Tex, a fine drummer and conga player; Chimp, beautiful time concepts; and Zap whose variety of skills with percussion, trumpet, synthesizing, vocals were awe-inspiring; and of course, Murph.

You want exciting, rhythmic feels? These guys could provide it!

I often wondered if John's initial reservations about the inclusion of "Wizard" came as a directive from Warner Brothers. In the end it didn't matter because we recorded the piece, and "Wizard" became the title cut.

Since it was named after Gandalf, the character in Tolkien's The Lord of the Rings, and because a new movie of the same name was soon to be released, "Wizard" seemed a reasonable marketing possibility.

After all was said and done, John got into it…and quite enthusiastically. We all, including John, were pretty happy with the results.

By my count, it took Matrix eight days to record and mix the entire *Wizard* album which, by the way, received a 4-star review in *DownBeat*.

I had read that a popular, heralded rock group took a *year and a half* to put together *their* latest recording. Hmm. Just saying…

# 55

After finishing the *Wizard* album, we were off to Kansas for the Wichita State University Jazz Fest, then on to Santa Fe, New Mexico. We finally landed at Scottsdale, Arizona for a date at the Double Tree Inn on April 26. The significance of this date was that our appearance was *not* booked by Willard, but by Bud Brisbois, world-renowned trumpet player.

He loved Matrix and, I suppose, used his celebrity stature to 'sell the band.' It was great fun as we hung out and got to know him. He threw a party for us at his house and even took a couple of us golfing.

At the party I had a kind-of brain fart, inadvertently referring to him as 'Bob.' As the drinks flowed, with much laughter at my expense, I remember having my arm around his shoulder and saying something like "Get my good friend here another Bobweiser!" Of course, he drank Bud.

In any case his total admiration of our music and our friendship with him would prove to be significant in the near future. From Scottsdale we tooled up to Santa Barbara. We had a play date at Baudelaire's where we had first heard Randy.

Randy was quite proud of Santa Barbara, his hometown, and with good reason. Accompanied by soft breezes off the Pacific Ocean, it's a lovely city, with an abundance of beautiful Spanish architecture. But *unquestionably*, the highlight of our stay there was meeting his parents.

Such cool, beautiful people! Bob and Lu (Lucille) were the most hospitable, caring people I'd ever met. They opened their hearts and home and modest backyard for a memorable 'cue (short for barbecue) featuring charcoal-grilled shark! Nothing was too good for Matrix!

A word about Bob's garage or, as Dietch called it, his 'Man Cave.' This was his hangout place, equipped with two TVs for both him and his sports-minded pals.

They would drink beer and check out the scores of various sports they enjoyed watching. There were pictures of jazz people, sports figures, multiple music posters etc. Particularly memorable was a life-size poster of Jaclyn Smith from *Charlie's Angels*.

It also featured a state-of-the-art sound system which piped continuous jazz (especially Matrix) when there weren't any games scheduled. Bob was never boisterous, always soft-spoken with a kind of half-smile on his lips. He was justifiably proud of his boy, Randy.

Lu was *everybody's* mom: always welcoming, smiling, and generous to a fault. What a pair!

After an unforgettable time in Santa Barbara, highlighted by the amazing hang at the Tico 'cue, we were off to Creston, Iowa for a second performance at Southwestern Iowa Community College.

From there we continued on to open for Woody Herman at the Civic Center in Eau Claire, Wisconsin. Then it was back to Lake Geneva, but not to record.

We were booked for a concert at the Playboy facility, a concert featuring—get this—Mel Tormé, Eubie Blake, and Matrix! Backstage I got to meet Mr. Blake and I actually got his autograph. A big 'yeah' there!

Then we headed to Madison for a one-nighter at a cool place called Bunky's. From there it was a short jaunt to

Rockford, Illinois for a couple of gigs at the famous Charlotte's Web, not far from Brad's hometown of Rockton.

It was late May when, thanks to Fred Sturm, now the Director of Jazz Studies (my old gig) at Lawrence University, we were invited to one of the most unique musical festivals we had ever experienced. Fred came up with a great idea and it was brilliant!

For the two-day festival, he brought in the following: international jazz composer Michael Gibbs, world-class lead trumpeter, our new friend Bud Brisbois, *DownBeat* publisher Chuck Suber, manager/booking agent, our own Dennis Justice, and jazz recording/touring group Matrix!

At some point on Friday, the first day of the event, he assembled us as a panel on stage to represent each phase of the music business. What followed was an amazing 'Q and A' about every aspect of the music industry from each of our various perspectives. Talk about an educational stroke of genius!

Here's Fred, a top musician, terrific composer, and fine director putting together a totally unique educational opportunity. There were clinics and rehearsals throughout both days, everything culminating in a whopping concert Saturday evening!

I will never forget the first half of the concert which featured Bud Brisbois performing on a piece Fred wrote: a musical tour-de-force that demanded all of Bud's considerable virtuosic skills. The last section called for Bud to switch from trumpet to piccolo trumpet. It was an insanely difficult piece, the last thing prior to intermission.

His performance brought the house down! People went crazy, screaming for more as Bud exited the chapel stage. I was getting chills as the audience kept up their enthusiastic approval!

Finally, Fred brought Bud back out on stage; he and the band then repeated the last section again! I never saw anything like it! An indelible, thrilling memory! Talk about 'a tough act to follow!'

Fortunately, there was an intermission which gave the audience a few minutes to process what they had just experienced and perhaps, to regroup emotionally.

On the second half of the concert Matrix was featured with the Lawrence University Studio Orchestra (symphony orchestra and jazz band). It was the proverbial 'cast of thousands' as people say.

This was special (for me at least) in two ways: one, I loved composing for Matrix and orchestra. "Childman of Ortelga," the actual piece we were playing, was inspired by the main character in the novel *Shardik* by Richard Adams.

And second, that night's performance was its *world premiere*. Talk about a memorable moment!

*   *   *   *   *

*An interesting sidebar to "Childman of Ortelga" was the manner in which it was realized: At the time, we were in the middle of a long tour when Fred called and requested that I compose something for his phenomenal event.*

*'Cool!' I thought. But hold on…this is going to take some serious blocks of time! When composing, I normally worked and 'thought' at the piano.*

*The trouble was, we were never in the same place long enough for me to sit down and write. The only long blocks of time we had were spent traveling from place to place.*

*The main area of the motorhome was usually a chaos of chatter, laughter, music on the intercom, etc. The only place with any privacy and relative quiet was…the claustrophobic little bathroom.*

*As a result, I spent hours and hours on the lid-down toilet seat composing the piece as we whizzed across the country (no pun intended). There were plenty of jokes as to the environment in which I wrote.*

*But regardless of the inconvenience of my work area, "Childman of Ortelga" turned out pretty well. In addition, the band seemed to enjoy playing it. I was happy.*

\* \* \* \* \*

Premieres have their own dimension of specialty. On that auspicious occasion after the performance, I especially remember what a warm, enthusiastic response the audience gave me as I stepped up to the microphone. I actually had to wait, and finally quiet their applause, before I could introduce the next piece.

There is no more meaningful reward than sincere appreciation of one's efforts; 'priceless,' as the TV ad says…and all of it dreamed up on a toilet seat!

# 56

Early on in our story, it was decided to mark the six-month anniversary of Matrix with a party at J.W. Puddy. The date was December 1, 1974. I remember it because I also quit smoking that day (cold turkey, I might add).

It then became our custom to throw an annual party as a celebration of our journey, our accomplishments, and our friendship. Of course, it made more sense to have our gatherings in the late summer or fall when we could all be outside.

Why outside? Because they were customarily bona fide pukers. No exceptions. So after the concert colossus at Lawrence mentioned earlier, it seemed the perfect time for the current year's event. Traf and I hosted the party at our house in Winneconne, Wisconsin.

May 29, 1978, the day after the concert, the celebration did indeed occur. It was a beautiful day. The weather was perfect. There was plenty of beer, and many people from last evening's performance were there, including our new pal, Bud Brisbois.

The party was rolling along nicely and the beer was flowing freely. Everyone was enjoying the buoyant afterglow of last evening's epic concert. *And*, of course, we were celebrating another milestone year of the Matrix ascension.

A pickup softball game on the ball diamond in the park across the street from our property added to the fun and festivities. *And* it helped dilute some of the effects of over-imbibing.

What I failed to mention in the previous chapter, was a situation that I hadn't anticipated. Prior to Matrix rehearsing with the Lawrence Studio Orchestra, someone suggested that Mr. Brisbois, double Tex's lead part...but *up an octave* during the climactic conclusion of my piece!

I agreed to give it a try and off we went. After trying out the idea in a run-through I kind of politely nuked the idea. (I don't think I was alone in my assessment). It was just too overpowering, negating some of the balance I had tried so hard to achieve.

Bud seemed cool with my decision and we all moved on. This is relevant to what follows. As the festivities of the party spiraled up, then eventually wound down, Bud and I ended up alone at our kitchen table. It was probably one or so in the morning.

He then shocked the shit out of me: "John, I want to be a part of Matrix!" The effects of a heavy dose of Stroh's beer quickly evaporated as though someone had doused me with ice water!

After the initial shock I mumbled something like, "Wow! Matrix, featuring Bud Brisbois!" Bud quickly countered with, "No! No! Not a feature; I want to be a *member* of the band!"

Oh boy...I didn't know what to say, or how to respond. For sure, I did *not* embrace the idea; my lame response may have betrayed my inner lack of enthusiasm. I remember little else of our conversation.

Bud was staying the night with us. The following morning, after warm hugs and goodbyes, he was off to the airport in his rental car. There was no mention of last night's conversation, everything perfectly normal.

So that seemed to be that, concluding one of the most memorable few days in my life with Matrix.

I believe it was Wednesday, two days later. We were still in bed around 8:00 a.m. when the phone rang. My wife answered, then handed me the phone.

"Hello John. This is Bud's brother-in-law..." (I don't remember his name) "We've got a problem here...*long pause*...last night Bud shot himself...."

I was totally dumbstruck! Blindsided!

He went on to say that when asked how everything went, Bud responded by saying that it was a disaster; that he had completely blown it, embarrassed himself! I simply could not process what I was hearing! This couldn't be! He was just in *our house*, we had just *talked*.

Oh my God! Could our last conversation have in some way contributed to his tragic exit? He *so* misrepresented his electrifying performance! I couldn't believe he'd said that! *He'd played brilliantly!*

This all seemed to suggest there were demons he was dealing with that none of us were aware of. To this day I still feel the aftershock of that god-awful phone call. I will always question if I might have had something to do with that tragic event.

Even now as I write this and, at the risk of sounding too melodramatic, I still can't help wondering...'What if?'

# 57

On one of our many Western swings, we once again skirted what could have been disaster. Regardless of the time of year, one should realize that traversing mountain passes (i.e. Rockies, Grand Tetons, Big Horn) the unwary motorist can suddenly be confronted with unseasonal snow.

And yes, count us as unwary. As we cautiously ascended one of the passes, snow began falling as the temperature dipped.

\* \* \* \* \*

*Keep in mind, none of us were experienced bus operators. I think there were four of us who volunteered to try and 'master' the demands of such a large vehicle. Oh, we all learned the art of double-clutching easily enough, but downshifting on an ascent was tricky.*

*In any case, we were slowly ascending and the light snowfall was making the road extremely slippery. I believe it was Zap, an excellent driver who was at the wheel.*

*I don't know if he just downshifted or not, but without warning the rear end of the bus started sliding dangerously to the right...toward the edge of the road!*

*I might add, there was a rocky drop-off of several hundred feet and this area of the road had no guard rail!! Zap had the good sense to try and brake, but in doing so, the rear end slid further to the right before we came to a stop.*

*We all got out and, to our collective horror, the back wheel was not more than five or six feet from the edge of this incredibly scary mountain drop-off! I guarantee, had we toppled off this edge…game, set, match; sayonara; game over!*

*The ass-end of the bus was angled precariously close to the drop-off and we decided on a plan, though I admit we were all scared shitless. Someone would back up the bus while the rest of us braced against the rear side of the bus nearest the edge.*

*If this didn't work, it was 'call 911' for a wrecker. Zap was the guy who stepped up, hoping to feather us back to a position of safety. His skill and, I might I add, courage with a capital "C", guided the bus to a position more parallel to the edge of the road. And at a much safer distance.*

*The fates, and Zap's mettle helped us avoid a serious tragedy.*

\* \* \* \* \*

Ah…ain't life on the road great?

# 58

It occurs to me that you, the reader, know very little about the individual players themselves other than from anecdotal references I've made along the way. These beautiful guys are what made Matrix special after all, so let me start by introducing the trumpet section.

"Tex" (Mike Hale) was our lead trumpet player, which meant he played a lot in the instrument's 'stratosphere', or the upper register. Considering the range of our library, a huge amount of musical 'heavy lifting' was put upon his very capable shoulders.

Tex got his nickname from having been born in Texas, even though he spent most of his early upbringing in Oklahoma. Other than music, I've already mentioned that he was wired in 'slow mode.' He rarely showed intense emotion, but if something bothered him, I'm pretty certain he internalized it.

As issues piled up to, let's say 'overload levels', he would finally approach me: "Chief. We need to talk." I learned to take these moments seriously. I knew he needed to vent, and as a fellow composer, his venting usually dealt with composition concerns.

As I may have said, he never complained much so I was always ready to listen when the invitation presented itself. This usually meant spending an off-night in a bar, both of us unwinding about the vagaries of composing. Before we became overwhelmed by alcohol he would speak with deep awareness, sensitivity, and humor.

I loved those vis-à-vis outings. They affirmed the old adage that 'Still waters run deep.' I admire his musical skills, his depth, humor, and his basic goodness as a person.

§

Then there's "Chimp" (Jeff Pietrangelo). You already realize his social 'pratfalls,' if I can call them that; the jokes at his expense that he seemed to willingly take, the totally laughable situations that he found himself in, etc.

But *don't* be fooled by the 'band clown' syndrome. When it came to music, he was a flat-out *genius!* I try not to bandy that term about loosely; I've not witnessed a more complete musician...ever.

His sight-reading skills were jaw-dropping, his technical mastery (chops) of the instrument was outstanding, his improvisational ability mind-blowing.

Perhaps most impressive were his musical instincts, particularly when we were working out concepts when putting a piece together. His suggestions always seemed so on-the-money, leaving me often wondering, 'Why didn't *I* think of that?'

He was always tasteful, creative, but never overbearing. Actually, quite the opposite, almost apologetic.

He was funny as hell when in party mode. I never fail to chuckle when I think of him slapping his considerable mid-section, admonishing his 'fat cells' as he called them: "Alright, alright! I'll get you something to eat as soon as we stop!"

One of the *funniest* things he created was 'Fast Face.' He would put both hands in front of his face, palms inward, sort of like the curtain on a proscenium. Then he would open the 'curtain' revealing say, a smile...the next opening might reveal a frown.

Gradually he would accelerate the opening and closing of the 'curtain.' Finally, in rapid succession, every time he would open the 'curtain,' we'd see a totally different face. Adding several beers to the mix, well—you get the picture.

The faster he went, the more hysterical we all became. I remember rolling on the floor once, laughing so hard that my sides *literally* ached.

Ah, Chimp. What was not to love about the guy?

§

The third 'chair' was held down by perhaps the most naturally gifted guy in the band. "Zap" (Larry Darling) was our Renaissance man; he did everything, and *everything* well! Not only did he play his trumpet parts accurately and musically, but he mastered programming the inscrutable Moog synthesizer and played exceptional solos on the damned thing.

I never did solve that beast, the synthesizer (If I was to play a Moog part, Zap had to program it for me). He also sang some of the gnarly passages I wrote, often doubling his vocal part with the Moog. Yikes!

Bear in mind that Zap is left-handed; he played all these parts with his *right* hand. So to his variety of skills I guess we could add 'ambidextrous.' We never used the 'lead singer' approach to our music.

We used the voice (or voices) as another color. Zap's singing ability and exceptional relative pitch kept him perfectly in tune with the often-unorthodox intervals I would write. What a luxury!

Add to that an amazing skill with percussion toys. And like Chimp, Zap had critical musical instincts! Our music was always open to many interpretations, so he added fresh ideas for us. He didn't possess the technical chops that perhaps Tex and Chimp had, but he would master his parts by dint of sheer hard work.

§

So, you've 'met' our amazing trumpet section. They collectively shared ideas with one another, were creative in their problem-solving, and weren't afraid to try out new ideas. As a composer, you can imagine what a blessing it was to write for these beautiful musicians.

# 59

The road can be a grind at times. Consider this: from July 7-28, 1978, the band played fifteen dates. *Fifteen dates in twenty-one days.* So, what's the big deal? Now consider this: from Madison, Wisconsin to Lafayette, Indiana to Champaign, Illinois for an afternoon gig, then back to Lafayette for an evening appearance; then to Chicago, Illinois, to Tulsa, Oklahoma, to Carbondale, Illinois, then to Cable, Wisconsin.

Carbondale is one of the southernmost cities in the impossibly lengthy state of Illinois. Cable, on the other hand, is about as far north as you can get in the state of Wisconsin. Them's a lot o' miles! Somewhere around thirty-one hundred and that's where the fatigue factor starts to wear on one.

Herb to the rescue! Thankfully, he set up a tape machine that piped tunes into the passenger area of the motorhome. As a result, we were actually able to enjoy the passing of miles rather than the drudgery of simply riding.

At that time, Fleetwood Mac was scorching the pop charts. In our tunneled life that really didn't matter at all, as we preferred the likes of Weather Report, George Duke, and Frank Zappa. One of our favorite albums was *Aja*, the newest release from Steely Dan.

On these insanely long trips, this musical diversion really helped make the miles fly by. But you know, nobody really complained that much. You got the dates, you went and played them. That's all there was to it.

\* \* \* \* \*

*Somewhere out west I think, we had a rare chance to do an afternoon rehearsal before an evening concert. We were working on a piece of mine, "Narouz," a character from The Alexandria Quartet.*

*It was a galloping tune in fast 3/4 with some tricky rhythmic phrases that Murph was having trouble with. Normally he nailed even the most complex passages, seemingly without effort. But for some reason this part of the piece had him hog-tied.*

*After our rehearsal we went to get something to eat at a Chinese restaurant. After finishing the main meal, the customary fortune cookies were served.*

*We were all reading aloud our random fortunes and Murph, a very funny guy, opened his. With a schoolboy-like straight face he "read" aloud…*

*"Don't play 'Narouz' tonight!"*

*The entire table erupted with laughter.*

\* \* \* \* \*

For me at least, performing our music was both challenging and fun! And I don't just mean my stuff. There were also wonderful pieces written by Fred, Tex, and Zap. I know of very few things that are as rewarding as playing high quality music, playing it well, and having 'said playing' appreciated.

Standing ovations became fairly routine, though I don't believe we ever took them for granted. They were affirmation of what we were doing. Validation: believe me, it meant *everything*.

Via the extensive booking through Willard, we generated a pot-load of money. As band members, we realized only a *fraction* of the take, but you know…it didn't seem to matter. What mattered, at least to me was, by god…*doing it!*

Looking back some forty-five years later, I now fully realize what deep collective dedication these incredible men demonstrated throughout our history as a band.

It's worth affirming again and again.

# 60

That stretch of fifteen dates in twenty-one days was child's play compared to our fall schedule. August 12 began a flurry of activity that, as I scan the itinerary, makes my head spin. It all started with an appearance at Chicagofest on the Navy Pier.

The gig itself was really unique; one I'll never forget. The bandstand was set up on one pier. Some 25-30 yards away, the audience faced us from the grandstand on a parallel pier. Having Matrix music floating over the water was pretty cool, far different from the usual auditoriums and stages.

As memorable as that was, it was an impossible venue to physically get *into*; and it was equally impossible to get the hell *out* of there after we'd finished our set!

As no one seemed to be controlling the traffic, it was absolutely agonizing since it took so long both coming *and* going! The gig went well but we were grateful when it was over!

A few days later we were back to Shade Tree in Lake Geneva, Wisconsin to start our next Warner Brothers album.

Now check this out: after five days in the studio, we boarded a very early flight to Telluride, Colorado for the festival there, played the gig on August 26, got up the next morning, and flew back to Wisconsin to finish up the recording.

I should note that my wife and son Jason had come along for this special event. On the plane ride Jason and Dietch both celebrated birthdays on August 27, and it was pretty cool that the pilot acknowledged their birthdays over the PA. We celebrated with cake and ice cream that Traf had brought along.

Jason turned eight, while Dietch just turned older.

Once again, it only took us eight days of recording for what turned out to be one of our biggest sellers. Yeah! *Eight days!* The album we recorded this time was *Tale of the Whale*.

I'll never forget Tex standing at the Oberheim synthesizer in his underwear, working out details of this extraordinary piece. He would labor over it seemingly for hours on end and, when he finally brought it to us, we knew we had a winner.

The title cut, "Tale of the Whale," was a beautiful piece of creativity that benefited from our 'collective method' of input from all the members of the band.

But it was Randy who 'put the icing on the cake'. Using his fretless bass with a Morley pedal, Randy created a most 'whale-like' sound by sustaining a deep, low pitch; while that first note was still sounding, and with his Morley pedal in the closed (off) position, he would then pluck the next note.

By letting up on the Morley pedal he could feather in the new note, connecting the new pitch with the first one in a seamless transition.

In this way, he was able to realize the melody that Tex had envisioned, creating a smooth, oceanic whale sound that was *totally* mind-blowing! To this day, I've never heard of anyone else doing anything like this!

During the *Tale of the Whale* recording session something else happened that should be noted: on the third day of the recording, an envoy from Warner Brothers showed up to 'oversee' our progress.

Ron Goldstein, the senior, most influential member, listened to a couple tracks. His very polite critique was less than reassuring. Then he revealed the *real* reason for their presence when he asked,

"Would you consider doing—let's say—a disco number; something we could market effectively?"

Aha. I got it...

I, also politely, answered by promising to proffer the idea to the band for a vote, knowing full well what the results would be.

The tally: Twelve 'Nays'; Zero 'Yeas'. Even the roadies and Herb emphatically said, "No way!" No sell-out here. Integrity intact. We all knew what this would probably mean to our future with the mega-icon Warner Brothers.

To a man though, we showed true solidarity and total commitment to our goals of creating high quality, challenging new music.

Period.

# 61

So, after the whirlwind: recording, flying, performing, back to recording—things did anything but slow down. From September 8, through December 13, we hit the following states:

Ohio, Indiana, Michigan, Wisconsin, Illinois, Iowa, Nebraska, Colorado, Montana, Utah, Nevada, California, Oregon, Washington, Idaho, back to California (six cities: Los Angeles, San Bernadino, Northridge, Lake Arrowhead, Garden Grove, and Santa Barbara), Texas, Louisiana, New Jersey (yeah, no misprint— Louisiana to New Jersey), Massachusetts, New York, back to Illinois, and finally Wisconsin...and home.

Whew! Twenty *different* states...that's closing in on half the country. I'm tired just writing it down!

Chimp always seemed to extend, at his own expense, an open invitation to some sort of cosmic humor. Although the guy could be funny as all get out in his daily self-deprecating antics, on this particular occasion, the gods of wicked humor seemed at play.

\* \* \* \* \*

*We were somewhere in southern California, I believe, when we stopped for the usual reasons: pit stop, stretch, get a soda, etc. After reassembling in the bus, we pulled out of wherever we were, heading toward the next destination.*

*Roughly fifteen minutes or so down the road, somebody asked, "Hey, where's Chimp?" Maybe asleep in the back? Nope.*

*Uh oh. You guessed right. He had been left behind. Naturally, we turned around and retraced our path back to where we had stopped earlier.*

*When we finally picked up the beleaguered little guy, he explained what happened. He was in the commode again, wiping himself (but not on his shirt tail this time), and heard the bus pulling away!*

*He scrambled as best he could (he may have even fallen down in his haste), but alas, it was too late.*

*Only to Chimp, it would seem, could such misfortune visit... God love him!*

\* \* \* \* \*

In the midst of this insane run there were a couple of notable events. We played Brigham Young University in Provo, Utah, for one of our higher paying gigs, $3,500.

To our utter shock and amazement, our management team then rolled up with a total surprise: they had just acquired a 1960 Greyhound bus which, by the way, featured eight bunks that Dennis and Phil had installed themselves! *Eight bunks!*

Personally, I've never been good at sleeping while sitting up, so this was a heavenly upgrade!

As you might imagine, none of us, except for Dennis, knew how to drive a stick-shift vehicle of this size. He had been a professional driver for the Stan Kenton Orchestra Unfortunately, he couldn't stay out on the road with us. As a result, some of us had to learn.

It's not the *easiest* thing to operate one of these beasts, believe me. This situation personally gave me a whole new meaning to the term 'double clutch.' It's a tricky technique you literally *have to do* in order to make the damned thing go! All in a day's work.

As far as drivers go, Zap, Tex, and Brad turned out to be the guys who would drive the bus until such time as we could get a pro. I had to give it up: I couldn't quite get the hang of down-shifting on an upgrade, and one time I stalled the damned thing on an uphill grade of a three-lane interstate.

I still occasionally cringe in the middle of the night thinking of what could have happened.

Fortunately, nothing did.

Back to the marathon tour. While in Los Angeles we played at UCLA; the next night we played at the famous club known as The Roxy. What made this noteworthy was the fact that Les McCann was on the same bill with us. Since he actually played first, I guess we could jokingly say, 'Yeah, we played The Roxy. Les McCann opened for *us*...' Right.

Also on this tour, we played and provided sound for an ill-fated festival in Galveston. Why do I say ill-fated? Because it was booked for Friday, Saturday, and Sunday of...(*oh boy*)...Thanksgiving weekend.

The promoter, whose name was Nick, was the same guy who'd run the Telluride Jazz Festival. He had booked an impressive line-up including such luminaries as Pat Metheny, Eddie Harris, Ron Carter, Flora and Airto, the North Texas State One O'Clock Band, and Betty Carter.

It may have seemed like a great idea, but... *Thanksgiving weekend?*

You probably know that Galveston is located on the shores of the Gulf of Mexico. You could hear the surf from the stage. Sounds ideal, right? The real problem was *that* particular weekend.

Nobody showed up.

I don't recall more than thirty to forty people for any of the concerts. To make matters worse, it got quite chilly after dark, with the ocean winds and all.

Let's think about this for a minute: wrong weekend, no people, cold nights…what else could go wrong?

On Sunday, the famous North Texas State One O'Clock Band was performing early in the afternoon. Winds began to pick up, menacing clouds started to gather…*uh-oh!* You got it: a total deluge hit us!

*Geez, our entire thirty-two-channel $100,000 Bose system exposed to the storm?!*

There was total chaos! People scattered. Cars got stuck in the sand; wind and rain came down unmercifully. Mud, wind, water everywhere…I mean, it was a complete disaster!

Everyone frantically scrambled to get the gear into the safety of the Moon Unit. We couldn't sit idly by and let our equipment get ruined.

*Herb was going nuts, shouting directions to us, collecting mikes, wrapping cords, hauling speakers…*

Our roadies were absolutely heroic! Everyone pitched in: musicians and roadies alike. Somehow, we got the equipment into the Moon Unit, all of those participating, drenched to the skin.

Once again, 'What else could go wrong?'

Well Nick, who obviously lost his ass on this venture, could only come up with about a third of the money we had coming. Of course, he disappeared, and we never heard from him again.

Ah, the glamor and bright lights of life on the road! No time to bemoan this disaster, we were due to perform the next day at Nichol State College in Thibodaux, Louisiana. We hauled ass out of there.

Another long drive...you get the idea.

# 62

I think now is a good time to leave the trail for a moment and introduce our beautiful trombone section: Fred Sturm, Kurt Dietrich, and Brad McDougal.

Of course, you've already met our first bass bone/composer genius, Fred Sturm. I have never met a guy with more positive attitude coupled with such wonderfully creative gifts.

After leaving Matrix, Fred went on to a distinguished career as a jazz educator: Lawrence University, then to the famous Eastman School of Music, and finishing back at Lawrence. But that's only part of the story.

He gained international recognition through his arranging/conducting skills with a series of German big-band recordings. His jazz compositions for young bands are played all over the country.

Watching him work with a band was magic; always the perfect metaphor, the perfect analysis, and always positive! I've never seen better. His contributions to Matrix were profound and remain with us to this day.

§

Now let me acquaint you with our lead bone player, Kurt Dietrich (deet-*rich*, not deet-*rick*) whom we always called "Dietch." He wore several important hats in the life of our band.

First and foremost, he played lead trombone flawlessly, often navigating devilishly difficult parts with apparent ease. He was a skilled reader and could handle damned near anything you threw at him.

But it was his silky tone that got me. Man, when a piece called for fluid lyricism, Dietch was the 'go-to guy.'

He also played background parts on our Oberheim synthesizer. Because of his keen pitch awareness, he was often called upon to sing vocal backgrounds that were often gnarly as hell, thanks to 'yours truly.'

Beyond Dietch's considerable musical contributions, he was what we laughingly called our 'treasurer'...*implying* that we had substantial amounts to disburse. No laughing matter to him though.

He kept impeccable books and issued our weekly, sometimes feeble, checks (Sometimes my check was as low as $30 for the week). A tough track at times, but Dietch handled the job graciously. Not an easy gig.

I should also mention his sense of humor which was subtle, and dry as the proverbial bone; no pun intended. He seemed to take a kind of perverse pleasure in calling out Chimp who, on one of his many diets, would sneak French fries from McDonald's onto the bus after a pit stop.

Dietch was a very well-read guy and, on the surface, may have appeared kind of bookish but underneath there was a sensitive, warm, fun-loving guy.

§

Then there was Brad McDougall, our bass trombone player *par excellence!* Brought up on a farm in Rockton, Illinois, Brad was both handy and hip. His musicianship was absolutely wonderful. He could sight-read anything, plus he had a big rich sound that was the rock-solid anchor for our ensemble passages.

Brad displayed an enviable air of confidence without ever hinting at arrogance. He tackled things head-on without flinching. If something needed to be done, he'd roll up his sleeves and *just do it.*

What a sweet combination: beautiful player, plus handy as all-get-out with mechanical issues. He just knew stuff about things which many of us had no clue. He also had a fresh sense of humor that, when on a long, grinding tour, was priceless.

He acquired the nickname 'Barry Schaefer', Schaefer being his beer of choice. And 'Barry' would sometimes morph into 'Barely'. Why? Who knows?

\* \* \* \* \*

*Barry had this quirky little ritual when finishing a can of beer. He would sit, holding the empty beer can horizontally at his knees, stare at it briefly and then…at warp speed:*

> *bang the can against his forehead,*
> *bring it back to his knees on its side,*
> *and deliver a karate chop to the helpless*
> *beer can…*

*He would then 'grade' the maneuver depending on how centered the blow was to the collapsed can. I know: pretty goofy stuff from such a bright, talented guy.*

*I guess that's what makes it funny as hell.*

\* \* \* \* \*

Aside from some occasional excursions into foolishness, Brad was well-rounded, easy-going, and likeable. Generous, intelligent, gifted…and you know what? On top of it all, he was model-like trim, and handsome, too!

What can I say? Some guys get it all.

Our unique instrumentation: five brass (three trumpets and two trombones) and one reed player called for keen sensitivity as to balance in ensemble passages. Dietch and Brad passed that test beautifully!

Not only did they anchor the group's sound, but they also achieved a wonderful musical blend with impeccable intonation.

The precision and balance of our ensemble became the signature of our "Matrix sound!"

These two guys were "as good as it gets!"

# 63

A couple of stops during our last tour were noteworthy. One was a three-nighter in New York City at a joint called The Other End, formerly The Bitter End. What made this gig especially interesting was the comedian who opened for us.

Though I don't recall much actual vulgarity in his act, he went by the name of 'Uncle Dirty' and was damned funny. Kind of old school, old pro. You definitely *knew* he'd been around.

We finished at The Other End on December 9, 1978. Two nights later we were at the downtown Holiday Inn in Chicago. We played Rick's Café American which was modeled after the famous nightclub in *Casablanca*. A very cool venue.

\* \* \* \* \*

*What made it truly memorable was that we each were given our own separate rooms! I always slept in my sleeping bag on the floor.*

*After months and months (actually years) of four guys crammed into one room, it seemed totally strange to find myself in a big, cushy, queen-size bed with no one else around.*

*After a bit, my room phone rang; it was Chimp calling to tell me that he felt weird being all alone. I get it...I know it sounds crazy, but I actually felt kind of...well—lonely too.*

\* \* \* \* \*

On December 13 we finally got back to Wisconsin and played Bunky's in Madison. A few days later our dynamic drummer Murph got married to Donna Enslow, the love of his life. As a present, I remember writing a piece for flute and piano which Kirch and I performed at the wedding. They both loved it.

It was called "Soaring…"

# 64

During the last marathon tour, we all knew that our tenure with Warner Brothers was probably over. I guess we thought this was all okay with everyone in the band considering their vain attempt to 'commercialize' us.

It may have simply been naïve idealism, but we didn't seem too concerned. Blind faith? I don't know.

Soon after the holidays it was 'strap it on' again. Everything started out benignly enough with a few regional gigs: Fond du Lac, Wisconsin; Cary, Illinois; back to Appleton, Wisconsin; and then…things got back to chaotic 'normal.'

One thing that certainly eased the stress of difficult, extensive touring was the hiring of Dave Scott, an actual professional bus driver! Dave, or 'Scottie' as he became known, was a cool California guy that Dennis knew, I believe.

What a blessing he was in terms of relieving pressure on those of us who had initially volunteered to help drive. I, for one, was *totally* grateful for Dave's presence.

Though I never minded driving the Moon Unit, I often volunteered for the job, especially if either Lauben or Randy was my navigator. Lauben was a great Green Bay Packers fan; and with my personal passion for the green and gold, Lauben and I could go all night talking Packers.

Another personal favorite was Randy Tico, nicknamed 'Speako' by Chimp. He and I both shared a similar multimedia vision for the band: Matrix performing with orchestras, dancers, slide shows, etc. We had a shared outlook: a passion/fascination for the theatrical.

Give us a six-pack and he and I could talk all night. His ever-positive outlook was contagious, and I always felt kind of uplifted after dreaming out loud with him.

When Dave Scott came aboard a great deal of pressure was lifted. Hell, there was pressure enough just performing our music every night…as well as doing it to the high standards to which we held ourselves.

# 65

Earlier I had alluded to our mutual disenchantment with mega company Warner Brothers. Something happened the last time we were in Los Angeles that totally disheartened us...*me*, in particular.

It turns out that Warner's jazz division was interested in adding the world-renowned Oscar Peterson, jazz pianist extraordinaire. I had studied piano with Oscar at the legendary School of Jazz in the late 1950's and established a lifelong friendship with him.

Mo Ostin, head honcho of Warner Brothers, called me into his office. I suppose he was interested in getting a reading on what I knew of the man. So, I'm sitting there and Mo asks me, "What kind of sales did Oscar's last album realize?"

I answered, "Somewhere between thirty to thirty-three thousand units, I think."

He scoffed, "Hell! Fleetwood Mac does that in a week!"

I thought to myself, *'We're talking about Oscar Peterson here.'*

And with that, Mo condescendingly wrote Oscar off like he was some kind of second-class citizen.

But then he went on to say something like, "You know, your so-called art music doesn't mean *shit* to me; you guys are a tax write-off for us!" Then, driving the dagger in deeper, he went on to say something like, "We target our entire recording operation to kids who are nine to thirteen years old."

*What? Was he kidding?!*

I was dumbstruck...blindsided...flummoxed...pissed off...and yes, hurt. I walked out of his office feeling as though my heart had just been ripped out.

I don't remember sharing the gist of that meeting with the band: way too painful. I mean, busting our ass, zigzagging across the country to perform and sell our beautiful albums, and then to have that kind of crap thrown at us?

Well, it was infuriating. And not a little disheartening.

So, what do we do?

We had a bunch of new stuff and some older things that we felt the need to record. I knew that Norman Granz owned several recording companies that included Norgran and Verve, one which later (I believe) became Pablo Today.

He was also Oscar Peterson's manager and initiator of the famous traveling group Jazz at the Philharmonic that featured an incredible clutch of jazz luminaries.

I remember that way back in January or February of 1976 a phone call came to our little farmhouse from Oscar himself. My wife answered because I happened to be in the bathtub at the time. She came to me with the message saying, "Uh...you just had a call from a Mr. Peterson...*as in Oscar!*"

Her eyes were as big as saucers when she told me he would call back which, in fact, he did. It was on that call that Oscar expressed how much he liked the music Matrix was doing. And Norman Granz, his manager was interested in recording us.

But Willard, who we had recently signed with, was working on the RCA deal and kiboshed the offer. If Norman was interested in us back in 1976, maybe he would still be interested now. I thought what the hell? What did we have to lose?

With Dennis and Phil's okay I just picked up the phone and called Mr. Granz. And to my total amazement he basically said, "Yeah! I'm still interested." I was flabbergasted!

Then he asked me what the sale numbers were on our last album. When I told him, he said something to the effect of, "My God, you do that with us, and I'll close up shop and take six months off in the Bahamas!"

He *did* say after asking me what it would cost, "Remember...I'm a jazz label and don't have the deepest pockets," or something like that. So, I kind of low-balled a figure and he went for it. Just like that we had a deal. Not even a handshake.

All done over the phone!

At the time, his label, Pablo Today, had no contemporary artists on the roster. However, he *did* have a stable of jazz giants: Oscar Peterson, Ella Fitzgerald, Joe Pass, Dizzy Gillespie, Buddy DeFranco, Terry Gibbs, Herb Ellis & Company—I mean, *come on.*

To be mentioned in the same company with those just listed...what a tremendous honor this would be for Matrix! And, it was all so old school the way it came down.

To this day, I'm still proud, as well as amazed, at how it all unfolded. It hearkens back to a time when a man's word meant something.

Long live Norman Granz!

# 66

As I mentioned earlier, Dave Scott, the bus driver, was a real blessing. He joined us on the January 25, 1979, and not a moment too soon! The reason I say that is because from that day in Stevens Point, Wisconsin, until March 23, we were hard at it.

From Wisconsin we headed for Bethesda, Maryland. On our way we were overcome by a bona fide blizzard and had to hole up at a roadhouse somewhere in Pennsylvania.

Murph, a sometimes head-strong Irishman, took it upon himself to cancel the gig we were supposed to play at a high school in Bethesda. No one objected and we had a great time 'snowed in' at a very warm, ambient lodge.

No one objected that is, *except Dennis*, who hit the roof! Dennis gave us holy hell for what went down! We laughed about it afterward but, of course, he was right...*tsk tsk.* (We still laughed though!)

Our life on the road was filled with excitement, adulation and the joy of music-making. But there's another side to all this, some of which we've already mentioned. On one occasion we narrowly escaped a dire tragedy.

\* \* \* \* \*

*Dave was driving us into Framingham, Massachusetts, for an engagement at the Bose facility. The day before there had been quite a snowstorm so roads were slippery.*

*I'm sitting about halfway back in the bus, speaking to Murph who had turned around to face me. We were just casually talking when I suddenly stopped in mid-sentence.*

*According to Murph, I had a look of horror on my face! We had just crested the hill and, at the base of it, I saw three cars stopped at a traffic light. The one closest to us was a VW bug. Oh my God!*

*Dave's left hand was on the steering wheel, an atlas in his right hand. I saw him looking down at the atlas instead of at the road.*

*Terrified, I shouted "Dave!" With unbelievable speed, Dave instinctively yanked the steering wheel to the right.*

*Thank God there wasn't a deep ditch, only a small swale. He followed with a rapid correction to the left, jerking the bus back so it was parallel to traffic.*

*He narrowly missed the three cars waiting at the intersection and ended up stopping a foot or so just past the traffic light.*

*Think about it. We would have crushed that VW and killed everyone in it. Just imagine the weight of a forty-five-foot Greyhound Bus laden with luggage and ten or so people.*

*I still wake up at night and shudder to think about what was miraculously avoided. And I am so grateful.*

*Dave was a damned good driver but had the unfortunate habit of steering with his left hand and consulting the atlas in his right.*

*Not everything on the road is glamorous.*

\* \* \* \* \*

Having recently received a sponsorship from Bose, the company invited us to perform a noon concert followed by a tour of their facility in Framingham, Massachusetts. Talk about impressive!

After witnessing first-hand, the infinite detail and care that went into the assembly of their sound equipment, I had a much deeper appreciation for the high quality and integrity of their product.

It's also why, with Herb's skill as well, we could sound so good whether we played outside or in a gymnasium. I know we were all extremely proud to be sponsored by such an amazing company.

I was quietly gratified to see their ad in *DownBeat* Magazine. It was a full-page shiny photo taken in the performance center at Berklee College of Music: Matrix surrounded by Bose equipment. Yeah! Classy.

That tour took us to North Carolina, Long Island, Pennsylvania, Illinois, Missouri, Kentucky, and Shelby County Prison in Memphis, Tennessee!

From there it was on to Denton, Texas (home of the famous North Texas State One O'Clock Band), Oklahoma, Michigan, Minnesota, and finally ending up in Lake Geneva, Wisconsin. There we went back into Shade Tree Studio to record Harvest for Pablo Today.

Looking back on that tour, as exhausting as it was, I can't imagine us doing all that performing, *and driving as well*, without Dave Scott.

People were always impressed and often amazed at how crisp and tight the band was. First of all, we had great players. Considering that the music was all memorized, and playing as much as we did, the results provided a pretty electrifying, jaw-dropping listening experience for our audiences.

In addition, the music we offered was so different from what was out there. As a result, we enjoyed a dimension of uniqueness admired by critics and musicians alike.

I recall talking with Bruce Paulson, a trombone player from the Stan Kenton band who, with a considerable note of envy said,

> "Man, you guys are doing what every player wants to do: create your own shit, record, and go out and do it!"

Some forty-five years later his passionate assessment has stayed with me.

When your peers dig what you're doing, that's serious validation!

# 67

For whatever reason, I've always had an interest in Native Americans. Growing up in the country, an eighth of a mile from a family of six mixed-blood kids may have had something to do with my leanings.

The mom was pure Chippewa or Ojibwa and the dad was Welsh, I believe. The kids *all* had wonderful hand-to-eye coordination and were much better at sports than I was.

But more importantly, they could tell when it was going to rain, when the fish would bite, when it was going to be hot, etc. Stuff like that made me envious. For example, the oldest boy, Ken, was an excellent marksman with a slingshot. Enviable at my age, perhaps nine or ten.

As I grew out of childhood, my attraction to Native Americans deepened and for a long time, I struggled to find a musical language that would reflect this interest.

This leaning ended up finding its way into the music I was composing.

After a few trials for the band (failures, I might add) I came up with some sonorities that resonated well with what I'd been hearing in my head. The result ultimately became the title cut of our next recording.

The piece was titled "Harvest." To this day, I confess to getting a bit teary-eyed when I hear the last section: 'Celebration Dance.'

In any case, one of the coolest things about this recording session was that we were once again reunited with our 'old' engineer friend, Andy Waterman. He knew us and our musical tendencies, so this created an ideal, warm setting for what can sometimes be a stressful experience.

No problem on that score. We'd been here before. He knew us, we knew him. All things good. And, in my opinion, all things *were* good.

We recorded a bunch of new things plus one truly 'old' piece: "Balthazar." That was the very first piece I had written for the 'good stuff' book, way back when.

Of all the new things we recorded, "Pony" was unfortunately never performed live. It was a kick-ass gallop of a piece! As I wrote it, I kept envisioning a mustang running wild.

That recording is the *only* thing that testifies to its existence. Too bad; it was an exciting burner.

Cover photography for *Harvest* is a powerful picture of a First American greeting the sunrise with a prayer; a feather in each upward-extended hand. For me, at least, it was very heavy.

You know the word matrix means 'mother' in Latin. It seems so appropriate because, as a group we essentially 'gave birth' to these recordings.

Up until then, the four albums we recorded were like our own children to all of us: like a mother with a bunch of kids, we loved each and every one for its own uniqueness.

Not that it matters, but Tim Schneckloth gave a four-star rating to *Tale of the Whale* in *DownBeat*. For our fifth album, *Harvest*, he actually came to my house, sat in my living room, and listened to the entire album…without a word.

After a long pause, he told me flat out, "This *definitely* gets five stars!"

Incidentally, *Harvest* was never reviewed by *DownBeat*.

# 68

You've already met all the horn players. On to the rhythm section.

Mike Murphy and Randy Tico were the most powerful rhythm section I'd ever been a part of, bar none! They created pockets of such electrifying drive, one would have to be deaf not to feel their pulse.

Before Matrix, my main concept of rhythmic feel came from the bop and hard bop tradition. Jazz rock, funk, and Latin jazz were pretty new to me.

In truth, these guys educated me big time! Plus, Zap, Chimp, and Tex were such great percussion players that I had to learn what *not* to play as well as *what* to play.

So, let me introduce you to these two.

Mike Murphy, or "Murph," and later, "Miff Murky," was one hell of a drummer. He was the driving force for Milwaukee's top funk group, Sweetbottom, led by Daryl Stuermer when we invited him to join us.

Sweetbottom was 'scary good' and Murph was certainly more than part of the reason they were so hot. Daryl, a brilliant guitarist, later became a member of the international English rock group, Genesis.

Murph was definitely fully Irish…without the brogue. Outspoken (you always knew where you stood with him) and blessed with a hilarious sense of humor. You may remember, "Don't play 'Narouz' tonight!"

Being Irish, he also knew what to do with a glass in his hand but I never saw him drink to excess. All in all, he was just so damned much fun to be around.

*And* he was also a die-hard Packer fan, so we always had plenty to talk about on those long trips.

\* \* \* \* \*

*One of the quirky things he always did when getting ready to play was to don the 'magic shoe,' a buckled boot/shoe with a substantially large heel. He would put it on the right foot, the one that handles the bass (kick) drum.*

*He said the shoe put his ankle at the perfect angle to most effectively execute the virtuosic rapid-fire 'kicks' which amazed us all night after night.*

*Murph's complete mastery of his kit, his innate musicality, along with his powerful beat, provided us the energy and drive that became an identifiable feature of the band.*

*Oh, and of course, his 'magic shoe.'*

\* \* \* \* \*

Then there was our bass player, Randy. As in "Tico."

Randy's 'chops' coupled with Murph's skills and dynamic energy took our rhythm to new heights. Together, Randy and Murph created a jaw-dropping level of exciting, powerful pulse that I, personally, had never experienced.

And, oh my stars, it was *fun!* Talk about grabbing a tiger by the tail! That's how I often felt when things got cooking.

Randy and Murph would often talk over how best to effectively emphasize the beat depending on the kind of piece we were doing. "Let's try this" or "How about this?" or whatever...on and on...until they settled on the best solution.

It was not only thrilling, but also enlightening and instructive for me.

And Randy, *as always*: "Maybe there's a better way…" But that was just him—continually striving for more, deeper, better. His positive attitude, his sense of urgency in expanding our concepts; *so* inspirational.

And let's *not* forget his totally beautiful solo concepts. He played some of the most lyrically exquisite solos on the fretless bass of any of the guys out there doing it. But, of course, when he picked up the 'fretted guy' for some funk… fasten your seat belts!

Man…he was something special. As if that wasn't enough, he was such a nice, humble, generous guy without a hint of egotism that so often plagues such talent.

For what we were musically trying to do, Murph and Randy delivered an emphatic 'mission accomplished' in spades!

# 69

On April 9, 1979, we finished mixing *Harvest* at Shade Tree Studio in Lake Geneva, had a week at home, and then were off again.

On April 18, we played the Blue Note in Boulder, Colorado. Two days later we were in Pasco, Washington.

From that point on until May 19, there were only two days off, one due to a cancellation. We played twenty-two gigs in a row that covered five dates in Washington, five in Oregon, and twelve from Weed, California (in the north), to Concord in south central California.

After that it took another three days to get to Mesa, Arizona. That's a boatload of 'hit and runs.' With that kind of a schedule, it's understandable how disoriented a person could become.

* * * * *

*I've always had a fascination for our national bird, the Bald Eagle. With our extensive travel, we often traversed eagle territory especially the Rockies or Northwest.*

*Never having seen an eagle in real life, I tirelessly scanned the skies for a coveted view of one.*

*One early morning, shortly after sunrise, we were in the Colorado Rockies heading in an easterly direction, I believe. Our driver, Scottie, Dietch, and I were the only ones awake.*

*I had my nose in a book when Dietch alerted me with an intense. "CHIEF!" I quickly looked up.*

*From the south, and to my right, a large golden eagle appeared. It flew directly in front of us, crossing our path as it headed north.*

*It was really close to the bus, perhaps twenty to twenty-five feet away. Setting its wings as it passed, it soared in a dramatic arc toward the east.*

*In an unbelievable visual I'll never forget, its huge wings and enormous body were gilded by early rays of sunlight!*

*I couldn't wait for our next stop so I could call home (no cell phones back then) to share the thrill of that unforgettable moment.*

*It wasn't 'Old Baldie' but that really didn't seem to matter. It was a breathtaking sight that I'll never forget!*

\* \* \* \* \*

To tell the truth, the most stabilizing moments (for me at least) were when we were performing on stage. Same basic setup, same wonderful guys kicking ass, same exhilaration during standing ovations, and then…tear down, get on bus, travel, get up in new town…

"What the hell day is it anyway?" Is it any wonder that we drank a lot of beer or that some did a little weed?

Nobody did anything harder than pot that I'm aware of. But come on; the human psyche begs for relief at times. If a few beers or a toke or two can provide that, so be it. No harm, no foul.

During one of those marathon tours, Tex found relief in a *most* creative cartoon centered around a duck. I can only describe it as a kind of collage with cleverly drawn hodge-podge characters.

He included cryptic inscriptions to define all objects that he had drawn. Written at all kinds of goofy angles, the quips somewhat cynically and comedically referenced the craziness of our traveling 'madness.'

I have always referred to this two page 'work of art' as the 'Quack Factor.' Seems fitting, don't you think?

Then there was our sound wizard, Herb, who was no stranger to, let's say…'escape mechanisms.' He came up with a pretty hilarious diversion on one long haul.

It seems he came into possession of a canister of helium. Instead of filling balloons or something, he filled his *lungs* by inhaling the stuff. He would then chatter away, his munch-kin-sounding voice at least an octave higher than normal.

I tell you it was piss-your-pants hilarious! He'd then pass the helium on to Lauben; same freaky, funny result!

Oh my! When you're dog-tired and road-weary, something like this was a welcome diversion.

We all know that laughter is a wonderful tonic with serious healing properties. Thankfully, there was no shortage of that commodity on *our* bus.

# 70

John Kirchberger, "Kirch" (rhymes with church), was the horn section's homogenizer, being the only saxophone player in the group. As an ensemble player, often his role was to play in the middle register between the higher-pitched trumpets and lower-range trombones.

He was also skilled on soprano sax (a higher register than tenor) so, as a result, he sometimes played the lead part. And then again, he was especially skilled as a flutist, both soprano and (*drool*) alto flute!

For those of us who composed, the keen versatility he provided gave us a wonderful range of options to choose from. In no way does this overshadow his brilliance as an exceptional improviser.

With his big, beautiful sound on the saxophone, his command of the harmonic language, exquisite time feel (beat) combined with technical mastery and creative genius as an adventuresome improviser, Kirch gave Matrix a powerful voice! A voice that drew raves wherever we played.

Perhaps even more important than his prowess as a musician was his gentle strength as a man. As a devout Christian his deep spiritual commitment had a calming influence when things got stressful. He never proselytized but, if asked, would readily discuss matters of faith.

What a blessing he was for us! His musicianship, his creativity, his sense of humor...his strength of character.

# 71

Thinking back, a full calendar year seemed much longer with our often-insane touring schedule. Maybe it was the distances we traveled, maybe it was the dozens of motels, the crappy meals on the run, the pressure of clinics and concerts…I don't think I'm alone in admitting, I'd often lose track of time.

But something I have *always* been grateful for (and still am to this day) was Herb and his crew. They were heroic!

We had a huge pile of gear to deal with and, considering the number of times they'd have to set up, tear down, pack up…perhaps you can see where I'm going with this.

Those guys did this night after night, always accommodating, never complaining. And…for poverty wages!

Sure, most of the time we would help with packing up after a concert, but come on: thirty-two Bose speakers, two sixteen-channel mixing boards (heavier than hell, I can tell you), electric piano, synthesizers, percussion stuff, mikes and mike stands, miles of cable to wrap, etc. etc.

Herb, Lauben, and Chris—those three will always remain heroes to me.

Herb's total understanding of our musical needs; his skill at bringing out the highlights, balancing the contrasts, caressing the sensitive parts; he was, *without question*, a critical tenth member of the band!

Whatever the venue, be it auditorium, gymnasium, night club, even football field, we all knew that 'sound-wise' we would be great. Having that kind of support from, and confidence in, the sound man…for a performer, it just doesn't get any better than that!

And then there were Lauben and Chris. These guys were tireless, accommodating, encouraging comrades. Equals in my eyes. Great pals in every sense, fun to hang with, always ready to answer your needs.

I think it takes a special kind of person to put up with the stress of our often-demanding schedule year after year. Any recollection of these guys has never failed to elicit warmth, laughter, admiration, gratitude.

In short…love.

# 72

By the summer of 1979, I feel it fair to say that our reputation in the music industry had grown to national prominence. Our albums were well-reviewed, they sold reasonably well for a jazz-related product and, *more importantly*, were enthusiastically received by our professional peers.

Matrix was awarded 'Performance of the Decade' from the Cultural Society of Yerrington, Nevada, for our performance on their concert series. Pretty heady stuff considering former recipients were the Budapest String Quartet and... Frank Sinatra!

And of course, earlier, we had received the Golden Feather Award as Best New Combo of the Year by the most iconic critic on the scene, Leonard Feather of *DownBeat* and the *Los Angeles Times*.

At the end of June, we played Summerfest in Milwaukee. Considering all the national attention we had received, I wondered how the home state would respond to our appearance. Our 4:00 or 5:00 p.m. time slot was prime and we were to open for the headliner, bassist Stanley Clark.

Walking on stage, we were blown away by what we saw. At the risk of sounding too hyperbolic, the mass of humanity packed into the audience area was mind-blowing!

Even all the lanes leading into the Miller Oasis were filled to overflowing. To be honest, though I'm loathe to make the reference, it reminded me of clips I'd seen of rock concerts.

Did we feel at all nervous? Or not up to the challenge? Come on…after all we'd been through at this point? No chance. We did what we always did: played a high-quality, ass-kicking show that brought about a thrilling, enthusiastic response from the overflow crowd.

It was estimated by some that the crowd was ten thousand, though I believe it easily could have been more! As I was approaching the microphone, I was thrilled by the sea of people packed into the viewing area! The piece I was about to announce was "Catalpa Complex," which I had written for my eight-year-old son, Jason.

\* \* \* \* \*

*When my little boy, Jason, was maybe six or seven, I taught him about trees and how to identify them. Due to its oversized leaves, the catalpa tree was the first tree Jason learned to recognize.*

*Should we chance to see one while driving or biking I would go into a goofy, mock 'freak-out' (spewing high-volume nonsense). We'd always erupt into unabashed laughter. Fun father-son stuff!*

\* \* \* \* \*

I was about to give my introduction when I spotted him, not twenty-five feet away in the midst of the throng. There was little Jason, perched on Traf's shoulders, sporting his new Donald Duck hat that she had just bought for him.

There was such an eager innocence in his eyes, emotion tugged at me and I was forced to pause, gather myself… or lose it.

I got a grip on my emotions and made the announcement, dedicating the performance to Jason. 'Sag a si nosaJ, nosaJ, nosaJ.' The inscrutable lyric is simply 'Jason, Jason, Jason is a gas!' … sung backwards!

It was a touching memorable moment that has stayed with me all these many years. Jason is now fifty-two with a seventeen-year old son.

You should know that a lot of thought was put into all of our performances.

Before each concert, Murph and I would sit down and plan the program. We intentionally chose pieces so they would gradually build in intensity, cresting at the end. And we got damned good at it.

Our performance that day at Summerfest was no exception. Whatever we programmed, it worked to perfection. When this humungous Summerfest crowd heard us play "Wizard," they went absolutely crazy! It was downright thrilling!

I'm telling you: we were no longer just a 'local band.' We were Matrix, by God! Matrix!

# 73

Shortly after our Summerfest (dare I say?) 'triumph,' we had our annual party back at our home in Winneconne (wouldn't want to pass that up; there *are* priorities, after all).

Then it was back to 'roll up the sleeves' with some very intense rehearsing for our next tour. Remember, we memorized all of our music, which requires a great deal of focus and concentration.

In other words, a hell of a lot of work!

Our first gig was another appearance at Chicagofest on August 9, 1979. It was followed by (*can you believe it?*) an impossible leap to Edinboro, Pennsylvania! And guess what? On August 12, two days later, we were back in Green Bay, Wisconsin.

Here we go again!

From Green Bay, it was a 'cream puff' drive to Minneapolis for an appearance at the famous Longhorn, a well-known jazz venue. From there the crew left for Telluride since we were hired to provide sound for the entire festival.

Herb and our sound system were once again making some noise in the music industry (no pun intended), thanks to the Bose company. I should add that the Telluride Festival was no longer run by Nick, the producer who stiffed us in Galveston.

Two significant events happened during the three-day Telluride Festival that are definitely noteworthy. Toshiko

Akiyoshi's big band was on the bill. Their manager came to us in a panic, looking for help.

It turns out that one of her trumpet players (fourth trumpet, I believe) missed the plane out of Chicago. They needed a sub immediately!

This was not the easiest request, mind you. I knew this because my close friend, Bobby Shew, had been in that band for a while and had complained about the difficulty of the trumpet book.

To his everlasting credit, our own Chimp stepped up and volunteered to fill in. His sight-reading chops (skills) were always mind-blowing to me. They would certainly be put to the test trying to navigate her stuff!

Well, he did just great, played well (no surprise there), and earned a nice check for his efforts (I particularly admired his balls for doing it as sight-reading was not my long suit).

It was one hell of a tribute to his all-around musicianship! Our loveable Chimp: a hero!

The other thing that proved to be significant at Telluride was meeting up with Flora Purim. She was the award-winning Brazilian vocalist in Chick Corea's Return to Forever. To my complete and utter amazement, she wanted to have *us* as her back-up band!

What?!? Hold on here. Flora Purim with Matrix? As zany as it may sound, it ultimately came to pass. But more about that later.

As I mentioned, we didn't go to *her, she* came to *us*. Flora loved the brass section and the rhythmic energy that we brought to the table. Her celebrity and all was a little overwhelming at first, but after getting used to the idea, it was pretty exciting.

Randy, for one, was euphoric; he *loved* the Brazilian influence from his upbringing in Santa Barbara.

## 74

So, from Colorado, we headed back to Wisconsin with visions of marquees reading 'Flora Purim with Matrix' or something to that effect. Of course, this would require some hasty arranging of her material, rehearsing with the band, planning sets, etc.

In the meantime, Dennis and Phil coordinated with Herb Cohen, Flora's manager, and started putting together a West Coast tour for us.

And if *that* wasn't enough excitement, Traf was getting really close to delivering our first child! As I revisit the drama, stuff was happening so fast it makes my head spin. Even today. Fun, exciting, scary times.

It seemed completely surreal to have an international celebrity descend on my provincial little village of less than 2,000. Flora Purim: jazz superstar, four-time winner of *DownBeat*'s Best Female Jazz Vocalist of the year. *Here?* In Winneconne, Wisconsin…population 1,935?

Let's see: huge glamorous city to tiny fishing village?

\* \* \* \* \*

*As the result of a mistake, Winneconne's 'claim to fame' came about in 1967 when it was accidentally left off the state map. Winneconne made national news when it 'seceded from the union,' declaring itself a sovereign state.*

*"Sovereign State Days" have been celebrated ever since.*

\* \* \* \* \*

It just so happened that we lived across the street from Lake Winneconne Park. Directly across the road from our house was a building simply known as The Barn. We ended up renting the place for next to nothing. Its size afforded a suitable space in which to rehearse.

And here's Flora, staying a block and a half from our house at the Wolf River Resort. The resort itself was, in fact, right *on* the Wolf River, but it was normally rented to fishermen. Talk about small town!

It was almost comical. We only had *one week* to put together our program! We were scheduled to play a full concert with Flora on Saturday, September 29, 1979.

Check this out! Just two days earlier, Traf gave birth to our son, Joshua Joel. Between hospital visits and rehearsals, I was pretty much a basket case!

I guess the concert came off okay, but I have so little recollection of the event that further speculation is non-existent. It's all just a blur.

But I *do* recall that Traf somehow convinced the doctor to let her out of the hospital to attend the concert. Some things you *never* forget.

Our actual tour with Flora didn't start for a few weeks so she flew back to California.

\* \* \* \* \*

*When Flora was in Winneconne, she and I were sitting and talking at our dining room table one afternoon. She was translating some Portuguese lyrics for me.*

*They obviously struck an emotional chord in her, as I remember tears streaming down her face. The deep sensitivity she revealed at that moment truly touched me.*

*During our conversation, as her tears flowed, she asked me if I might be interested in an arranging gig. She wanted me to score the pieces she had talked about…for orchestra. When I readily agreed, she thanked me and that seemed to be that.*

\* \* \* \* \*

After our debut concert with Flora at Pickard Civic Auditorium in Neenah, Wisconsin there was a bit of a break. I was really grateful; it gave me a little time to figure out how to begin to be a new dad.

# 75

Our upcoming tour would pretty much cover the West Coast all the way from Oregon to Arizona. Before heading out, the few days we had off were kind of heavenly, considering what was in front of us. Flora Purim and Matrix! It was an exciting prospect for us...time to try on this new look!

On October 20, we met up with Flora for a concert at Humboldt State University in Eureka, California. Things seemed to be going okay for the next few dates but, to tell the truth, it seemed to me that the crowds were more interested in hearing Flora than us.

She was still quite a draw, but it was different. After all, she was the *centerpiece* of the show and we were simply the backup band. It *was* a unique experience, albeit quite a different role for us.

When I stop to think about it though, the audiences that came to hear Matrix were quite different from the crowds that came to hear Flora, the star of *Return to Forever.*

After all, remember that she was voted best female vocalist in *DownBeat*'s annual awards. She was also the very same femme fatale who did time for possession of narcotics. You get the picture.

She had a following of devoted fans, and we were pretty much an afterthought. No matter. We were making money and had a pretty cool itinerary to look forward to, especially two dates at the Great American Music Hall in San

Francisco on October 25-26, 1979. I loved that place because of its storied history. I mean, anybody who was *anybody* in the jazz world played the Hall. Besides, it was the venue where we first heard about Randy Tico.

The first night we played there, happened to fall on my birthday, October 25. I don't recall anything out of the ordinary about the gig except receiving a great framed picture of Duke Ellington. I think it was from Lauben, or maybe the whole band. I don't remember.

After the night's performance, we agreed to a rehearsal and meeting the next afternoon. So the next day we met as planned, expecting to go over some of her charts, etc.

Nary a note was played; Flora arrived...sparks flying, guns blazing! She proceeded to rip everybody a new one!

Somehow, I was spared, but she pretty much tore everyone else apart for at least half an hour.

We were all dumbstruck! What the hell happened to this pleasant person who enlisted us as her band? The scene was truly bizarre! We were totally blindsided! And we still had a bunch of dates to do to finish the tour.

So, *this* was what it was like to back up a celebrity?

It wasn't clear, but either before or after her blow-up, she apparently called her famous percussionist/husband, Airto Moreiera; perhaps even some of the band members from her recent album, *Carry On*.

She was, after all, coming to her home turf and possibly felt some misgivings about these Midwest guys playing her music.

During our second night there, Airto, Keith Jones (bass), Hugo Fattoruso (keyboard), and Flora played a couple of tunes by themselves. And in truth, the guys who sat in were beautiful, and we thoroughly enjoyed their playing.

Flora was cool as though nothing had ever happened, and the rest of the night went without incident. Unfortunately, the explosive scene from the day before still left me, at least, feeling a bit uneasy.

Our next three dates were in Los Angeles.

# 76

Whatever Flora's issue was, we headed into Tinseltown with less than an abundance of confidence. The first of those dates was at UCLA, a gig definitely in our wheelhouse, you might say. You know…college crowd, enthusiastic response, the type of venue in which we had flourished dozens of times.

No issues. We've got this!

Then, there were two nights at The Roxy in downtown Los Angeles. There would be a horde of Flora's adoring fans and the strong possibility that some of the musicians who recorded with her would be there.

After San Francisco, Airto stayed on tour with us. I think it was our first night at The Roxy that he invited brilliant trombonist, Raul de Souza, plus a couple of Brazilian percussion guys to join us.

On my part, I confess to a hint of anxiety; that is…until we started playing! Oh my!

The time feel was exciting as hell, believe me! Their percussion and ours melded together resulting in a kind of 'super-feel.' Talk about exhilarating! Any angst about these guys joining us evaporated, replaced by a rhythmic excitement that was memorably mind-blowing!

*And* these guys were both nice and gracious. A good lesson learned here: anxiety, a subtle form of fear, has a sinister way of paralyzing the free-wheeling, creative process.

True story: During a newspaper interview, I was once counseled with the following truism: "If you worry you die; if you don't worry you die; so why the hell worry?"

\* \* \* \* \*

*One of the coolest moments while in Los Angeles with Flora, was not on the band stand, but in the parking lot of the Hollywood Hotel.*

*It was there that I actually met 'the Kid from Red Bank,' or you may be more familiar with his celebrity name: William 'Count" Basie!'*

*I saw him heading to his car sporting his famous nautical Captain's hat, just boldly walked over to him, and introduced myself. Any concerns about my possible intrusion on his privacy were quickly dispelled.*

*In the few minutes we chatted, he couldn't have been nicer and actually seemed flattered by my overture. That moment is a real treasure in my personal memory trove.*

\* \* \* \* \*

Back to the tour which, regrettably, turned out to be our last.

Airto stayed in Los Angeles after our last night at The Roxy. We only had a few more appearances left on the tour that included a night at The Catamaran in San Diego.

Two nights later, on the first of November we concluded the 'Flora/Matrix collaboration' at a place called Dooley's in Tucson, Arizona. Nothing out of the ordinary, no issues. No drama.

There was sort of a 'let's-get-this-done-with' kind of vibe. Mission accomplished. And so ended the less-than-rewarding though life-expanding experiment.

What did we take away from this? We were probably both better off doing our own thing.

# 77

As our somewhat unusual tour with Flora was winding down, storm clouds were brewing on another front. The source of this unease centered around Seventh Mountain Management.

I'm being totally honest when I say that I am hazy when it comes to details during this brief chapter in our existence.

I *personally* thought, and *still* think, that Seventh Mountain had the near-impossible task of booking and guiding a nine-piece, forward-looking, classically influenced jazz group. No vocals, no guitar! But this I *do* know: they believed in us!

Flora's manager, Herb Cohen, was in charge of dividing the money. After taking his commission, he paid Flora, then Matrix.

In any case, some of the band members (probably me, too?) felt that we were coming out on the short end of the stick, so a few guys decided to be proactive: they took it upon themselves to go to Mr. Cohen and voice their concerns.

He sent them packing in no uncertain terms. "I *never* talk to musicians. *Ever!*" Mr. Cohen then promptly called Dennis and Phil and read them the riot act as well.

A word of explanation: when an artist signs with a manager, like a marriage, it's a relationship totally based on trust.

According to Dennis...we violated that trust.

In defense of those who ended up going to Mr. Cohen's office, they *unquestionably* had the band's best interest at heart.

Heaven knows that throughout our journey we had serious financial hardships. If there were any doubts about the inequity of the money breakdown, I believe we were justified in at least trying to get some clarification on that issue.

In Dennis's words, however, we committed the *cardinal sin*.

He and Phil got in the car, drove to the beach, watched the ocean…and quietly wept.

After a short time, they drove back to the office in silence and drew up a letter legally terminating our relationship.

# 78

I don't have a lot of answers, but I do have a lot of questions. For example, *did we actually think we could manage and book ourselves?*

Dennis, in particular, had knowledge, skill, contacts, and experience from years with Willard as one of his most prolific agents!

Phil, one of Stan Kenton's former bass trombonists, was the business administrator. He took care of contracts, royalties, negotiations, and was totally honest by the way!

Another question: *what the hell were we thinking?*

While the rest of the band members headed home, I was the signatory for Matrix business and had to return to Los Angeles. It was my job to sign off on our severance with Seventh Mountain Management.

I remember clearly that after signing the appropriate documents, Dennis and Phil drove me to the airport. Little was said. It was gut-wrenching; a Samuel Barber "Adagio for Strings" moment.

During the ride I felt weighed down by the finality of it all—the painful realization that there was something special that had 'been'...that would be 'no more.'

After a tearful farewell to Dennis and Phil I got on a plane for Wisconsin. Normally this would be a moment of joyful anticipation. Not this time.

I flew home burdened with the dull ache of a heavy heart.

Why is that feeling still so poignant...even today? After all these years, it still hurts.

# 79

It wasn't long after our Matrix journey was over that the phone rang and, to my utter surprise, it was Flora! She had approached Allyn Ferguson and Jack Elliot, co-directors of The Orchestra and secured a commission—*for me!*

(Remember that conversation we had at our dining room table back in Winneconne? It had spoken volumes as to her sensitivity *and* generosity.)

She asked me to score a suite of three Brazilian songs for her, accompanied by an orchestra. But not just any orchestra; *The* Orchestra!

It was founded in 1968 as an artistic channel for film and recording studios' most gifted musicians. This was a 'dream combination' that included The Los Angeles Philharmonic Orchestra and stellar jazz musicians like Bud Shank, Jerome Richardson, Bill Watrous, John Audino, Ray Brown—you get the idea.

I embraced the commission with gusto and finished the score fairly quickly. But then came the grunt work: part-copying.

I couldn't afford to pay anyone else to copy the parts, so I set to work. Because of the enormity of this task, we'd had to place extra leaves in the table to make it as large as possible.

Normally, on the appropriate part, I would simply write 'first alto' or 'lead trombone'. *But no—that wouldn't do.* For all of the jazz and studio players, Mr. Elliot specifically told me to write each person's name on their part: Bud Shank, alto sax and flute; Bill Watrous, trombone; John Audino, trumpet; and Ray Brown, bass…etc.

Damn. That was one heavy responsibility for me. This was big time stuff!

I worked almost nonstop on part-copying for roughly two-and-a-half weeks but I also had to play gigs at night. I wondered how in hell I was going to be able to get it finished. Somehow, don't ask me how, I finally managed to get all the parts copied.

Exhausted, I looked at the time: 3 a.m. The next morning my wife came downstairs and saw the table, completely covered with stacks of parts!

Then she saw me. Face down on the table… fast asleep.

My next problem was how to transport all that music. I found a large enough suitcase in which to neatly arrange each part. Luckily everything fit. As I left for the plane, I almost felt as if I should padlock it to my wrist, sort of like an international courier.

Flora arranged for me to fly to Los Angeles for all rehearsals and the performance. After all was said and done, everything turned out quite well. The performance was great. It was well-received and, most importantly, well-reviewed.

When the time came to return home, I felt rewarded and well-paid. This was an *august* moment in my arranging life. This experience came with a heavy responsibility, but I shall always be grateful to Flora for the opportunity.

I might also add that it truly overshadows any darkness that may have occurred with Flora at the Great American Music Hall back in October.

# 80

Back home in the Midwest, Matrix booked a few regional gigs a couple of weeks later. The first one was at Calvin College in Grand Rapids, Michigan where our dear friend, Derald DeYoung, was teaching. He was an accomplished trombonist and superb teacher who had taught at Lawrence University in the 1970s.

Derald had pretty much mentored all our brass guys when he taught at Lawrence. That gig was an especially joyful reunion for all of us.

The next night we once again returned to Charlotte's Web in Rockford, Illinois. The date was November 17, 1979.

Why is this date so significant?

Well, it turns out that Matrix would *not* play another gig for twelve-and-a-half years!

I know, I know... *What the hell?*

I don't recall who initiated the meeting, but that night after the Charlotte's gig, we gathered. As I remember, Chimp seemed to take the lead. Someone suggested some time off.

I looked around at everyone, my comrades. Heads were down.

When Chimp posed the question, "After a month or so, does everybody agree to reconvene?" heads nodded silently... less than enthusiastically, I thought.

Then Chimp turned to me, "Chief, you okay with this?" Without hesitation I responded "Yes." What the hell? Is water wet? Is the sky up? This is Matrix! *Of course I was in!*

We departed, embraced, even joked a bit. I kind of knew in my heart of hearts, this may have been our last…

…in discussing this book with Dietch he recently confided his reaction to our last infamous meeting so long ago. In his own words, he said: "*What?!! Break up?* This is what we *do!* "

He went on to say, "I had trouble imagining no band. But that's what happened."

We'd come so far, and against such daunting odds, and in such a relatively short time. But to be honest, the rigorous touring schedule had taken its toll. Burnout was written on everyone's face, including mine.

Okay, let's take a little time off. Regroup. I'll write some new material. Come back reinvigorated, right?

The reality was that three of us, Murph, Dietch, and I had gotten married during the course of our story. Then came kids, and…life at home was *wonderful!* It was becoming harder and harder to think about leaving…

You get the picture.

And, oh yeah…we no longer had Dennis and Phil to put us in front of all those fans. As the saying goes, "All good things must come to an end." (I *hate* that cliché).

I'm fully aware that I am an incurable romantic, but it still pains me to realize that we had clawed our way to notoriety and frankly…let it go.

# 81

Twelve-and-a-half years seems enough time to "regroup," "reinvigorate," etc. In 1992, Dietch's wife, Maria, was Director of the Green Lake Music Festival.

She gave me a call offering a commission to create a piece for Matrix. She wanted to feature us at their annual event. I was stunned!

Everyone had gigs, day jobs, families, etc. If by some miracle everyone was available, I would do it in a heartbeat!

Turns out everybody was in! They all cleared their schedules and what do you know? Game on! So, I got to work right away. The commission turned out to be a lengthy tribute to Miles Davis, which I titled "Proud Flesh," the title cut of our last album.

Musically, it was meant to highlight several phases of his profound career. I got this crazy idea to select quotations from his autobiography and then incorporate them electronically at appropriate places within the music.

By this time, Zap had taken over all the recording responsibilities at Lawrence. I went to the Lawrence studio and, paraphrasing some of Miles's quotes, *spoke with a gravelly voice*. With a little studio processing, it sounded close enough to Miles for my purposes.

Ultimately, we all gathered, including Herb and Lauben, to put this thing together!

And get this: Steve Patton is a close friend and band director at West High School in Billings, Montana. He drove all the way out to Wisconsin by himself, *solely* because of his admiration for Matrix.

He offered his services in any capacity just to see the band close up, and to witness how we worked. Another set of hands couldn't hurt so he became a gofer/roadie. The band quickly embraced this easygoing, likeable guy.

He proved to be very valuable and helpful to Herb and Lauben.

We had to learn new music and put a full program together without much time to do it. For several days at the Lawrence University rehearsal facility, we worked like hell to pull this off.

I was euphoric! All of us back together making music… Matrix music!

It was like waking to a dream! It was unbelievably cool! I recall occasionally choking up during rehearsal just thinking of this amazing group; old memories flooding in…

And the capper was that Bob Tico, Randy's dad, flew out from Santa Barbara to be a part of this event! What an incredible, joyful reunion this was!

We ended up playing three gigs through the Green Lake Festival which we jokingly referred to as our 'World Tour.' We premiered "Proud Flesh" for our first concert in the Alberta Kimball Auditorium of Oshkosh West High School. We then played an outdoor concert at the Performing Arts Center in Milwaukee, and finally ended the 'tour' with an *outstanding* concert at the storied Pabst Theater.

There was such a rekindling of memory and joy, the result of being together again! Sort of like your long-lost, loving dog showing up at your door. This all came to pass, thanks to Maria (and Dietch, I'm sure).

I would be remiss if I didn't recognize my dear old friend, Barney Apthorp.

Remember that he hosted a party at the Milwaukee Hotel after our performance with the Milwaukee Symphony. He then sent money along with me to celebrate after our Monterey performance.

Once again, he stepped up and threw a wonderful party for us after our Pabst Theater gig. Some people never learn! *Thanks, Barney!* May he rest in peace.

# 82

We were invited eight years later to be the headliner at the Neenah Jazz Festival (later renamed Fox Jazz Fest). As this was the millennial year, it was a big deal.

Matrix performed on September 2, 2000, to an overflow crowd of truly enthusiastic fans. The weather was perfect. And it was so great just to be back together again making music.

Matrix music.

\* \* \* \* \*

*Celebrations were planned all over the world for the new millennium. At the same time there were also major concerns. Due to the large increase in the use of digital information during the 1990s, would the computerized infrastructure be able to adjust properly?*

*There was actual fear. What would happen to computer grids and systems all over the country…or the whole world for that matter?*

*When the date changed from December 31, 1999, to January 1, 2000 , would everyone, and particularly businesses, lose all their data?*

*Fortunately, there was a seamless transition and everyone relaxed as the new year began.*

\* \* \* \* \*

*Proud Flesh*, a tribute to Miles Davis, was so enthusiastically received that we absolutely *had* to get it recorded. Sometime in 2001, we decided to put together a full album that included two other Matrix composers besides me.

Larry Darling wrote a lovely little piece called "Branches" that ends the album. He also wrote "Fast Face" and "No, Seriously." And Mike Murphy wrote a joyfully buoyant tune called "Festival City."

To help create an authentic 'street sound' for Murph's tune we needed more percussion to add color and excitement to this exhilarating piece. We asked Dane Richeson, Director of Percussion Studies at Lawrence University, to record with us since he had plenty of access to an extensive variety of 'percussion toys.'

Another issue that came up: Kirch wasn't able to attend all the rehearsals because his dad had just recently passed. We solved that problem by enlisting the stunning talents of Tom Washatka on tenor saxophone.

Tom has a big, beautiful sound, could read anything, and was a hell of an improviser. He was an absolute perfect fit. Talk about saxophone colossus with these two titans, Kirch and Tom, side by side!

We also invited Oshkosh guitarist and local legend Tom Theabo to join us. (Hey! Finally a guitar!) This truly helped lend an authentic street sound to Murph's "Festival City."

One also needs to remember that Tex hadn't played lead trumpet in years so would understandably need some help. With that in mind, we also asked legendary trumpeter, Al Johnson (formerly of the Count Basie Band) to help with some of the lead parts.

We were lucky that he was available and readily agreed to help us. These additions certainly enhanced the production of this new recording project.

And also, my dear friend, Tom Washatka, brought his saxophone to play alongside Kirch. These additions certainly ramped up the excitement level for Murph's piece. Chimp, who was playing a lot on the Milwaukee scene, took care of a number of lead parts (especially on *Proud Flesh* itself).

The recording took place in the jazz rehearsal room at Lawrence, which had a direct feed to the recording studio. Once our project was finished, everything was fully mixed and ready to go.

Okay. Now we had the recording. What do we do with it?

We considered Stellar Records, owned by Tom Washatka and Janet Planet as one option but we were hoping for a bigger label if at all possible.

By chance, Dietch attended a jazz educator conference and happened to be introduced to Kip Sullivan, a representative from Summit Records. In chatting with him, Dietch began to talk about the recording Matrix had recently made.

Mr. Sullivan was quite receptive to the idea of taking on a finished product. All they would have to do would be the pressing and packaging. Summit agreed, and the rest is history. The result: our last studio release, *Proud Flesh*.

As of this writing, it is still currently available through Summit Records.

Then in 2002, Matrix was invited to perform at an outdoor concert called the Northern Aire Jazz Festival near Wisconsin Rapids. We appeared on the same stage with Nicholas Payton and Count Basie. Talk about being in good company!

For this concert, we again enlisted the superior talent of Tom Washatka and Chimp continued to play lead parts on *Proud Flesh*.

And *finally*, on September 5, 2009 (geez, won't these guys *ever* leave?), Matrix was featured as the headliner at the Fox Jazz Fest, this time at Jefferson Park in Menasha, Wisconsin.

This is an utterly gorgeous park along the edge of Lake Winnebago. What a phenomenal setup! The shoreline is lined with lovely shade trees and the stage faces the lake. An absolutely idyllic setting!

From the stage, Matrix had an incredible view of the 3,500-plus people in attendance: people in their lawn chairs, boats anchored offshore, the sparkle of sunlight on the water...what a stunning visual for our artists to be inspired by.

As artistic director of the festival, I received numerous raves from the performers about the physical beauty of our setup.

According to festival staff, our Saturday-only performance drew more people than the *combined two days* of any year in their twenty-five-year history.

Word had gotten out that Matrix was to be the headliner band and a crowd filled the park like never before.

We were greeted by a wildly enthusiastic crowd when we walked out on stage. It appears that Wisconsin was still proud of its unique home-grown phenomenon.

# 83

Up to this point it occurs to me that I've said very little about the unique music Matrix was presenting. The actual music we played was completely new and different from what was going on out there at the time. It could be described in the most general terms, like "challenging," "forward-looking," etc.

In the musical world we were navigating, journalistic criticism was just part of the game. Almost totally from the reviewer's perspective, a career could be boosted…or cruelly cut off at the knees.

You only need to read a couple of reviews from Nicolas Slonimsky's *Lexicon of Musical Invective* to realize how short-sighted, self-centered, and downright wrong critics can be!

However, in the hands of an effective critic even a negative review often contains *constructive* criticism. An occupation that wields such power in determining an artist's career demands an effective knowledge and the fullest integrity of the reviewer.

§

John Wilson of the *New York Times* wrote:

"The band's repertory, made up of entirely original material—most of it by John Harmon, its keyboard player—is a mixture of the brassy sonority and occasional pomposity of Stan Kenton and the kind of airy impressionism that Gil Evans created in the 1950s, when he was providing settings for Miles Davis.

On the record, the two contrasting styles and sounds are brought into balance that is *so* effective that the final result is a distinctive style that can be identified as Matrix's own."

He continued:

"There are brass ensembles for three trumpets and two trombones that are beautifully shaded and full of rich colors. Mr. Harmon's arrangements make interesting use of voices to expand some instrumental passages."

§

In an article called "The Sound of Surprise from Matrix," Leonard Feather of the *Los Angeles Times* wrote:

"It would be a disservice to use the term jazz/rock in analyzing this fascinating orchestra. Its scope is too broad, its level of artistry too high, its potential too great for such pigeonholing...

Most of the material is written by Harmon, who plays keyboards, and by trombonist Fred Sturm. Between them, they cover an amazing range of textures, colors, tempos and moods, changing *so* often that the sound of surprise is never more than seconds away."

He continued:

"A tremendous creative effort clearly went into the building of a library for Matrix. The result is a band that cannot fail to appeal to the emotions, the intellect or to any jazz enthusiast who, tired of bebop clichés or rock overkill, is receptive to something adventurous, exciting and just about totally new."

I'd spoken earlier about our goals and it appears we achieved them. When two tough critics of both knowledge and integrity sincerely sing your praises...can you blame us for feeling pretty good about our work? I believe those reviews pretty much validated our musical worth.

For the record, I'm damned proud of all of us.

# 84

My deep gratitude and love for those that have passed will be with me for the rest of my life. However, I would be remiss if I didn't honor those who are still with us.

§

Tony Wagner, our first drummer, took me in when I separated from my first wife. We lived together in a small upper apartment in Appleton. He was instrumental in helping me determine the personnel of Matrix, but unfortunately, left the band early on. I shall always be grateful to him for his help and encouragement.

After leaving Matrix, Tony earned a degree in Phy-Ed and taught at the high school level for a number of years. He also continued his musical career as co-leader of the very popular band Street Life.

Married with two grown children, Tony is now retired from teaching and lives on a beautiful little lake in Waupaca, Wisconsin.

§

After Matrix, our tireless lead trumpet player, Mike Hale (affectionally called Tex), took a job as band director with the Appleton School District, retiring in 1997. He is also a confirmed bachelor.

His selfless, take-one-for-the-team role as lead trumpet is still amazing to me. Playing so often in the stratosphere of the trumpet's range had to take its toll, but I never heard a single complaint. He knew that this was his responsibility, and he embraced it...*in spades!*

Because Tex always played lead, one had the tendency to overlook his considerable skills as an improviser. When given the opportunity he could weave absolutely *beautiful* melodic lines.

Having perfect pitch, he contributed to vocals *and*, with his consummate sense of time, could also greatly enhance percussion parts as needed.

Talk about your all-around guy. Thanks, Tex.

§

And then there's Zap, Larry Darling. I've spoken of his incredible versatility already. But his many skills aside, what sticks in my memory the most was his fearlessness. He'd try anything!

He seemed to have complete trust in his abilities and would just go ahead and 'do it.' From a 7/4 solo ("Childman of Ortelga") to scream-singing the coda to "Harvest" (way above his range), to easing the bus down a dangerous slope back to safety...

He once said to me, "I've heard of a program taking civilian passengers into space. If there is such a thing, I want to be in on it!" (Something close to that). That's Zap.

After working at Lawrence University for twenty-three years, Larry retired from his position as recording engineer. He now lives/travels with his friend, Pat, and their cat and dog: Harvey and Ruby.

§

Ah, Kirch. John Kirchberger, this wise and gentle soul, had a wonderfully calming effect on us if things got stressful. Soft-spoken and caring, he was (and is) a devout Christian, but was never preachy.

Obviously, his technical mastery was stunning! His beautiful, improvised solos, huge sound, and virtuosic chops (technique) were *so* inspiring! I'm talking about alto and soprano flute, and soprano and tenor saxophones; he was equally skilled on *all* of them.

Most importantly (for me at least) is how beautiful he is as a human being! I know we are all blessed and made a little better as people because of him.

§

And then there's Dietch, Dr. Kurt Dietrich. They threw away the mold after he was made, that's for certain. I've already spoken of his silky-smooth lyricism, but he could get aggressive if the musical situation called for it. *New York Times* critic John Wilson said this of Dietch in his review, "Matrix Plays Jazz at Other End":

> "…Kurt Dietrich's trombone is particularly eloquent, not only as a dark ensemble color, but in a solo piece, "Come September," in which he brings great warmth and tenderness to an attack that, on other occasions, has something of the brusqueness that Bill Harris showed with Woody Herman's Band."

In addition to his outstanding musicality, there's a strength of character that needs to be mentioned: Dietch was probably the most even-keeled, objective guy in the band.

When things got stressful (especially over financial woes) he'd quietly go about his treasurer duties, never letting on about our somewhat gloomy financial situation. Perhaps he internalized stuff, but you'd never know it from his demeanor.

I remember feeling sorry for him as he apologetically handed us our meager checks during a lean week. The complexity of our finances: band checks, motel payments, past debts, gas, Willard, Seventh Mountain Management, vehicle upkeep…he took care of all that and never once complained.

That quiet strength will always be a quality I admire.

He has a wonderfully dry wit, is very well-read, and has authored several books: *Duke's Bones: Ellington's Great Trombonists* (1995); *Jazz Bones: The World of Jazz Trombone* (2005), *Wisconsin Riffs: Jazz Profiles from the Heartland* (2018); and his latest, *Never Givin' Up: The Life and Music of Al Jarreau* (2023).

Dietch has two grown sons and is now Professor Emeritus of Music at Ripon College, Wisconsin, where he taught for thirty-nine years.

The image of this rail-thin young Virginian picking up his trombone and breaking your heart with sweet simplicity will be what I remember most.

§

Brad, or Barry, or Barely, McDougall was our bass trombone player who replaced Fred Sturm. I actually like what I had said earlier about his being both handy and hip. His farm upbringing provided him knowledge of mechanical things well beyond any of the rest of us.

He was such a fine musician with great reading skills and, in ensemble passages, had the perfect big sound to anchor our horns. I recall how easily he fit in when he first joined the band, a testament to his very likeable personality.

He carried himself with such upright confidence without any hint of arrogance. He, like many of our guys, had a wonderful sense of humor!

\* \* \* \* \*

*I believe it was Brad who bought a nine-inch-tall Big Boy doll when the bus stopped to eat at one of their restaurants. He painted its brown hair black like Chimp's (including protruding nose hairs) and hung it on the curtain runner.*

*This chubby little guy looked way too much like a caricature of Chimp for any of us to miss the reference.*

\* \* \* \* \*

Brad recently retired from building custom homes with his brother for the past twenty-eight years. He continues to play bass trombone in both the Knoxville Jazz Orchestra and the Knoxville Symphony Orchestra.

§

And then there's Randy. I think I run the risk of unabashed hyperbole when discussing his beautiful musical gifts. I can honestly say I've never played with a bassist quite like Randy; his skill level was simply jaw-dropping! His positive attitude and energy still jump out at me.

Rehearsals, and especially recordings, were so revealing as to who he *truly* was. "I think we've got one more take in us…it could be that magical one…" etc.! We'd all be draggin' ass but Randy always thought there was another 'discovery' waiting to be tapped into.

And some of the, let's say, impassioned discussions between he and Murph were truly enlightening. It was something to behold as they bandied their opinions and ideas on the appropriate approach to a particular passage.

Once they'd settled on a concept, it was killer! Guaranteed!

A performer, composer, and producer, Randy currently lives and works in Santa Barbara, assembling large-scale multimedia projects for the Santa Barbara Arts Festivals and others.

§

No way can we forget our first bassist, Randal Fird. He tended to lean a bit toward the reclusive, often with his nose buried in some esoteric book that only *he* might find of interest.

Essentially, Randal was a deep thinker. He was soft-spoken and gentle, and pretty easygoing. He didn't talk a lot, but when he did, it would more than likely be something worth listening to. As a player he was rock-solid. And as a soloist he had a lovely, lyrical gift. We all loved Randal.

After leaving Matrix, Randal lived in Boulder, Colorado where he worked for thirty-some years as a mechanical designer. Now retired, he enjoys hiking, camping, and traveling with his wife, and considers himself a world traveler/ explorer.

§

Michael Bard was the original saxophone player with the band. I've spoken earlier of his authoritative 'leader mentality' that was unfortunately a poor fit for the rest of us. Rather than a single person leading the band, we *all* contributed to the whole; we were a collective.

There was still a lot to admire about the guy though. He was a fine player on many levels: sight-reading, chops, sound quality (especially on soprano sax). He was blessed with fine musicality and was also a unique improviser.

Personally, I loved his great sense of humor (he introduced me to Monty Python's *Flying Circus*)! Obviously, our separation wasn't fun, but those wounds have long since healed.

After Matrix, Michael went on to a very full, productive career. He recorded, toured with the Stan Kenton Orchestra, and with the Simon and Bard Duo. He now runs his own business: Studiobard, a highly efficient, full-service digital video/audio production and original music studio.

He lives in Portland, Oregon, and is married with two grown children and two grandchildren.

§

Dennis Justice could easily appear intimidating; he was six-foot-two, had a large girth, and was roughly 285 pounds with a full head of hair and well-trimmed, *full* beard. His speech was measured, never hurried.

Socially, he was jovial, generous, fun-loving...a kind of big, lovable bear. On the surface one could be fooled by his seemingly casual persona. *Forget it!* This cat had more street savvy than anybody I'd ever met!

I suppose years of driving the Stan Kenton bus around the country, and years in the stable of Willard Alexander Agency afforded him not only a hard look inside the game but especially how to play it!

This adventure of ours would never have happened were it not for *one* chance hearing by *one* particular man: Dennis Justice. The electrifying jolt he got from what he heard one afternoon, along with its musical power, gave him a passionate belief in us that ultimately got the ball rolling.

Over time, I came to love the man; a man who put his entire career on the line for us.

After Matrix, Dennis drove tour buses with people from all over the world. At the age of 56 he formed his own company (starting with just one bus) and built his business up to a fleet of 48 buses and 55 employees.

He now enjoys retirement and, in particular, his 13-year old son, who is also named Dennis.

§

Ahhh ... Lauben (Doug Lautenschlager). Here's a guy who is both *smart* as well as street-smart. Under Herb's guidance he became an indispensable *super-roadie.* He was obviously a quick study in mastering the complexities of our setup. "Anything you need, Chief?" I've heard that hundreds of times throughout the dozens of tours we did.

When it was my turn to drive, I always loved it when Lauben was my 'navigator' because of his observations, sense of humor and, something we both shared: a passionate allegiance to the Green Bay Packers.

He will always remain an endearing, loveable member of the Matrix family. A friend for life.

# 85

Fast-forward to the present. It's 2022 and I'm looking back. What did we do? *And*, how did we do it? Good questions.

What we did was create a body of quality, original music that was both fresh *and* challenging. Nothing that I am aware of, before or since, resembles the unique approach to music-making than that of Matrix.

It was an ensemble that effectively explored an expansive range of emotions from the gentle "Come September," "Clea," "Blue Snow," "Branches," to the dynamic, electrifying "Maestro" (a tribute to Aaron Copland), "Earth and the Overlords," "The Last Generation," and "Pony."

By combining voices with electronic and/or acoustic instruments, Matrix introduced new colors that produced, at times, haunting effects.

Without going into great detail, we also did a lot to expand the scope of our listening audience. Much of what we played was programmatic: musical storytelling based on imagery.

For example, as the composer, it was my job to introduce "Wizard." I'd prepare the audience by telling of confrontations that would occur between the hobbits and the evil dark riders known as "Nazgûl" from Tolkien's *Lord of the Rings.* This prepared the audience for what they were about to hear.

Zap created musically evocative, electronic space-age sounds *ala Star Wars* on the Moog synthesizer. Multiple percussion layers by other band members added to the chaos, suggesting frenzied battle scenes. The rest was up to the audience and their imaginations.

Other examples of our programmatic repertoire could also be found in "Tale of the Whale" where Randy's bass suggested an undersea environment by creating the deep rich sounds of a singing whale.

And "Nessim," an introspective character from *The Alexandria Quartet*, was musically portrayed by an exotic four-voice vocal background. Beneath the voices, a repetitive, Egyptian-sounding bass pattern gave the piece an alluring, haunting mood. Chimp's searing Harmon mute passages gave further evidence of the character's intensity.

To this day, close to fifty years later, I continue to hear from people affirming the positive influence Matrix had on their lives. Critics across the country gave us universally high praise. But the *ultimate* affirmation was from our peers; musicians who *totally* admired what we had accomplished musically.

The thing is while we were out on the road performing night after night after night, I *knew* we were good. I would guess that sometime in 2019, Randy Tico sent me a live recording: the 1979 Matrix concert at Lawrence University.

Oh, my stars! It was only then that I realized *just how good* we were!

After all that time, objectivity fully intact, I listened in total amazement as we romped through our program. It included, by the way, the very demanding "Wizard," with many gnarly passages to execute.

The performance was remarkably clean and crisp…*flawless!* There were no punch-ins here (the term for inserting

a corrected note into the studio recording). No retakes...
this was *live!*

By performing so much together, I think we pretty much
took our playing for granted. But I can tell you...hearing it
after so many years, it was jaw-dropping *phenomenal!*

This may sound like a boast but check it out for yourselves.
Go to the Matrix home page: http://www.matrixjazz.com/

So, the short answer to Question Number One: What
did we *do?*

We did a lot. Much of what Matrix offered could be
qualified as 'timeless'...as relevant today as it was back then.

§

Question Number Two: How did we *do* it?

The easy, obvious, and short answer was through a lot
of hard work. But that merely scratches the surface of the
*full* answer.

Most likely you're familiar with the concept of: 'The total
is more than the sum of its parts.' It's a concept that, in part,
certainly explains the Matrix phenomenon. Our collective
*most assuredly* added up to more than the individuals in it.

Each member's unequivocal belief in the *integrity* of what
we were doing cannot be understated. The magic was created
through the total heart-and-soul investment in our ideal.

Oh, we had our standout individuals, no question. But
*together*, we were one *hell* of a formidable voice!

*The intangible dimension that made us unique was the love
we had for each other.*

No cliché here. The bonds forged by exhilarating tri-
umphs, bitter disappointments, exhaustive schedules, bad
food, crummy motels, laughter, tears, great performances,
less-than-great performances, etc.; all of these created life-
long friendships like nothing I've ever experienced.

By now we've lost several of our Matrix family: Herb was the first to go. Then Murph. Then Chimp. Chris. Fred. Gary...It hurts like hell to even think about these losses.

Thankfully, the pain is somewhat eased by the many wonderful memories they left behind.

# 86

As I conclude this book, I confess to a bit of sadness. Sifting through the sands of memory, my nostalgic leanings make it difficult to exit, having so thoroughly enjoyed the process.

But before I take my leave, please know how deeply humbled and blessed I am to have been a part of this extraordinary group of creative men.

Those six plus years, the Matrix years, had a huge hand in shaping me as a human being.

Something I read perhaps forty-five to fifty years ago became a personal mantra for me. The reference is from Antoine de Saint-Exupéry's *The Little Prince*. The character of the fox gives the Little Prince a spoken gift:

*"It is only with the heart one can see clearly;*
*what is essential is invisible to the eye."*

When I reflect on the Matrix journey, I can unequivocally declare—*from the heart*—I dearly loved the creative life we were living...

beating the odds...

chasing an ideal...

Above all, I will always love that brotherhood of gifted, dedicated men who *so willingly* shared in the chase.

For this memorable chapter of my life, I will always be deeply grateful.

# Afterword

Although it is not at all obvious from the narrative of this book, the real hero of the book—and the story of Matrix—is John Harmon.

When I wrote *Wisconsin Riffs: Jazz Profiles from the Heartland*, I got a little carried away in profiling my dear friend and mentor, and John's profile ended up being one of the longest in the book. Not that it wasn't deserved. I won't relate all of his story here, but I will give the thumbnail version of his life and career before the advent of Matrix:

Born in Oshkosh, Wisconsin, 1935; started playing piano by ear as a kid, sometimes playing duets with his mother Polly; off to Culver Military Academy in Indiana for high school, where he would furtively listen to recordings by Art Tatum at night after "lights out"; entering Lawrence College in Appleton to study music, even though he could barely read music; working bars and clubs as a college student; after graduating from Lawrence in 1957 attending the School of Jazz in Lenox, Massachusetts during the summer, meeting and studying with jazz giant Oscar Peterson; playing bass drum in a service band, while honing skills with other like-minded jazzers in his unit; going to New York to be a musician, leading to a recording with the esteemed Yusef Lateef; months of steady work at a bar in Bermuda; a long USO tour of American bases in Europe; moving to Buffalo, New York, where he earned a master's degree in composition (studying with famed composer Henri Pousseur) and had a steady duo gig with future Tonight Show bassist Joel DiBartolo; moving back to Wisconsin, establishing a working trio and eventually being hired to teach jazz at Lawrence University (which is part of the reason he moved back in the first place).

After all that was recounted in that incredibly long sentence is when the story in this book begins. What is missing from John's account of the Matrix saga is just how crucial he was to the venture, from its initial conception until the very end.

I'm not sure that I completely buy all of the details of his story of the germination of starting a band. But then I tend to distrust any story that's set in a bar in Wisconsin. I did not hear of the idea until quite a few months later, when, as I recall, I got a call in Evanston, Illinois, where I was attending graduate school at Northwestern University.

Like the others involved in this "merry band" dream, I had only the foggiest notion of what I was going to do when I was done with school. So Matrix it was.

As I look back, one of the comical aspects of getting some of the guys into the band was something like "parental approval." What were the parents thinking could possibly go wrong with a group of nine guys running around the Midwest playing music in bars? The really humorous part of it was that some fears were allayed because "at least Mr. Harmon will be with them." If only they knew.

But musically, it was a different story—eventually.

At its inception, Matrix was playing a lot of "radio tunes." We were playing Chicago, Blood, Sweat & Tears,

The Beatles, Stevie Wonder, you name it. Pretty much all of the horn players were copying charts off records. Fred Sturm was making beautiful original arrangements of some of them. I'm sure that John was doing some of this; I think he had done a little chart on Herbie Hancock's "Chameleon," and probably others.

But he already had his eye on the eventual goal, which was to have a band playing its own music. He was already writing originals. I know that one of the first of his compositions we did was "Balthazar," which we continued for the whole history of the touring band, finally recording it on our fourth album, *Harvest*.

Soon we were playing some originals by other members of the band, while continuing the radio tunes, so that we could keep working. Fred was, of course, a mighty contributor to the "original" book. We put two of the movements from his huge work *Childhood's End* for Matrix and the Milwaukee Symphony Orchestra on our first album.

We played a number of compositions by our first reed player, Michael Bard. Larry Darling's lovely little "Blue Snow" was on the first album. Fred's gorgeous "Spring" was on the *Wizard* album, and Mike Hale's unique "Tale of the Whale" was the title cut of our third album.

But the vast majority of the pieces we ended up playing were John's originals. He set the musical direction in which Matrix traveled. That's not to say that the rest of us didn't offer plenty of suggestions about his pieces once he brought them to us. Hardly a single one of the pieces survived the scrutiny of the rest of the band without some changes.

Changes for the better, I'm sure John would say.

In the "mature" days of the band, bassist Randy Tico and drummer Mike Murphy especially brought some great ideas about rhythmic feels to the pieces. Some changes evolved naturally; Larry added synthesizer parts, the guys added percussion, and so forth.

But they were John's pieces. And there were outstanding musicians (and some of us who just were able to carve out our own niches), and some superb soloists in Matrix; John was at the top (if not alone there) of the list.

Ultimately, Matrix was John's musical vision. After the long interval since we quit touring (*forty* years!) it's difficult to have the perspective to look back and realize that a five-and-a-half-year touring life, even in the glory days of the live music scene of the 1970s, was a pretty amazing run. The band was carried by the remarkable camaraderie of its members and crew.

But John, who I still call "Chief," from those days, was the rock of the whole operation. Every member had his own role, but Matrix was his baby. No John Harmon, no Matrix. A high point in all of our lives.

Hail to the Chief.

—Kurt Dietrich
Ripon, Wisconsin

# Acknowledgments

My heartfelt thanks to Dr. Ross Tangedal, Cornerstone Press, and his wonderful editorial staff, including Brett Hill, Kirsten Faulkner, Ellie Atkinson, and Grace Dahl. Their keen eyes and sensitive suggestions were a godsend and greatly appreciated. Thanks, also, to the press production and media teams for their contributions to the book, in particular Carolyn Czerwinski, Zoie Dinehart, and Nat Reiter. I am also honored to offer deep thanks to my dear friend Matt Buchman who, after reading the manuscript, put it in the hands of Dr. Tangedal.

Profound gratitude and deep love to Jeff Galloway for his life-long, continuing support of jazz and jazz musicians in the Appleton/Fox Valley area.

Most importantly, to my loving wife, Traf (Linda), for her amazing commitment and editorial skills in seeing this project to its completion. Without her love and support, the book would never have been written.

JOHN HARMON is a widely commissioned composer, having written music for the Milwaukee Symphony Orchestra, "The Orchestra" of Los Angeles, the Fox Valley Symphony and the Santa Fe Chamber Orchestra. He created the jazz studies program at Lawrence University in Appleton, Wisconsin, and later founded and led the award-winning jazz nonet Matrix, which toured the country for nearly six years.

Harmon serves as Composer-in-Residence for the Red Lodge Music Festival, artistic director for Fox Jazz Fest, teaches in Door County at a jazz fantasy camp for adults, and in 2005, he was named a Fellow of the Wisconsin Academy of Science, Arts, and Letters. He holds honorary doctorates from Lawrence University and Ripon College.

Born in Oshkosh, Wisconsin, he lives in Winnecone, Wisconsin, with his wife Linda (Traf) Harmon.

www.ingramcontent.com/pod-product-compliance
Lightning Source LLC
Chambersburg PA
CBHW021714120626
4654SCB00004B/1551